INTELLIGENCE
ITS EVOLUTION AND FORMS

INTELLIGENCE,
ITS EVOLUTION AND FORMS.

GASTON VIAUD

*Professor of Psychophysiology
and Director of the Laboratory
of Animal Psychology Strasbourg*

SCIENCE TODAY SERIES

GREENWOOD PRESS, PUBLISHERS
WESTPORT, CONNECTICUT

The Library of Congress has catalogued this publication as follows:

Library of Congress Cataloging in Publication Data

Viaud, Gaston, 1899-
  Intelligence; its evolution and forms.

  Translation of L'intelligence.
  Reprint of the 1960 ed., issued in series: Science today series [ST-1]
  Bibliography: p.
  1. Intellect. I. Title.
BF431.V513 1973   153.9   72-10983
ISBN 0-8371-6640-3

BF
431
.V513
1973

Translated by
A. J. POMERANS
from *L'Intelligence* first
published in France

© *English translation Hutchinson & Co. (Publishers) Ltd., 1960*

Originally published in 1960
by Harper & Brothers, New York

Reprinted with the permission
of Harper & Row, Publishers, New York

First Greenwood Reprinting 1973

Library of Congress Catalogue Card Number 72-10983

ISBN 0-8371-6640-3

Printed in the United States of America

CANISIUS COLLEGE LIBRARY
BUFFALO, N. Y.

CONTENTS

	page
Preface	9
Introduction: General characteristics of intelligent actions	11

Part One
PRACTICAL INTELLIGENCE

1 The Intelligence of Animals	25
2 The Practical Intelligence of the Child	41
3 The Practical Intelligence of Adult Man	55

Part Two
LOGICAL AND RATIONAL INTELLIGENCE

4 Conceptual Thought	71
5 Logical and Rational Thought	88
Conclusion	114
Appendix	119
Select Bibliography	121
Index	123

PLATES

	facing page
Chimpanzee Experiment	32
Ant-maze Experiment	33
Octopus Experiment	64
Rat Experiment	65

PREFACE

THE word 'intelligence' has several meanings. It may refer to 'intelligent' as opposed to instinctive and automatic behaviour, it may refer to the faculty of understanding, and it may equally well be used as a yardstick of mental capacity. In other words, when we speak of intelligence, we mean either certain *modes* of behaviour and thought, or else a certain *level* of mental agility.

The determination of the level of man's intelligence is called psychometry. This is a field we shall deliberately ignore since it merits a volume on its own. If we do mention levels of intelligence in animals and children, it is only because their very investigation has led to a deeper understanding of these types of intelligence.

We shall be mainly concerned with intelligence seen in its evolutionary perspective, a problem that concerns both philosophy and general psychology, each in its own way. The philosopher considers intelligence to be one aspect of the mind. He tries to define its nature, and studies its relationship to life and matter. The psychologist is more modest in that he is content with describing those forms of thought—or activity—which we call intelligent and with discovering the laws which govern them. While this book is written from a psychological point of view, we shall nevertheless point out some of the philosophical applications of modern psychological findings.

We shall be guided throughout by a notion that has a direct bearing on all problems of intelligence, and that has played a paramount role in experimental investigation, viz. the notion of *practical intelligence* introduced by Bergson some fifty years ago. Before that time, philosophers and psychologists recognised only the rational intelligence of man as it appeared in logical analysis, and the instincts of animals as they were observed by naturalists. They completely ignored what Dr. Pierre Janet (*Intelligence avant le langage*) has called the *terra incognita* between instinct and intelligence; psychologists of fifty years ago knew no more about that region of the mind than did 18th century explorers about the African interior.

Today we know better. The practical intelligence of apes and children has been investigated, and to a much lesser extent that of *Homo faber*. But even here, the spadework has been done, and the result is of such importance that the psychological investigation of tool and implement-making has become an integral part of the study of intelligence.

INTRODUCTION

GENERAL CHARACTERISTICS OF INTELLIGENT ACTIONS

Instinctive and intelligent actions

Philosophers have traditionally contrasted instinct and intelligence. Although this distinction has often been taken to extreme limits, it is a useful starting point for defining the crucial characteristics of intelligent actions.

By 'instinct' we commonly mean a predetermined and automatic response to given external stimuli; a response, in other words, that is inborn and that need not first be learned or acquired through training. Simple examples are *reflexes*, and *tropisms*.

We need spend little time on reflexes, which are the direct and immediate *motor* responses of effectors (muscles or glands) to external stimuli. Their study belongs to the laboratory proper, reflexes being characteristic of physiological processes rather than of overt behaviour. Tropism, on the other hand, must be considered to be a real, if inferior, type of animal behaviour. The term tropism was first used by Loeb for orienting (and movement) responses to physical and chemical agencies. The best known form is phototropism, or movement towards a source of light. Such behaviour, however unthinking and mechanical it may be, is the motor response of the *entire* animal, and not of an isolated limb or muscle. The intensity of the phototropic response varies directly with the intensity of the source of light. Thus, a butterfly will fly more quickly and more directly towards a stronger than towards a weaker source. In short, the influence of tropism is such that it will cause an animal to behave like a mechanism which, while subject to anatomico-physiological factors, is set off and kept going by external forces. This type of behaviour is characteristic of Descartes' so-called 'animal-machine'.

A higher class of instinctive reactions is *avoidance* (and defence-reactions) and its opposite: the *approach* impulse (cravings or appetites).

Let us look at the case of approach impulses, such as hunger and sexual desire. A hungry animal will roam about as though under a compulsion, and, having detected the presence of food, it will move inexorably towards it. Here the intensity of the response no longer depends on the intensity of the stimulus, but on the degree of privation. Clearly internal factors have become more important than external stimuli.

Instinctual, i.e. biological, drives are characteristic of much of the behaviour of animals and also, if to a lesser extent, of man. This point was illustrated most eloquently by William James, when in his principles of psychology he wrote:

'Why does the hen, for example, submit herself to the tedium of incubating such a fearfully uninteresting set of objects as a nest of eggs, unless she have some sort of prophetic inkling of the result? . . . Why do men always lie down, when they can, on soft beds rather than on hard floors? . . . Why do they prefer saddle of mutton and champagne to hard-tack and ditch-water? . . . Why does the maiden interest the youth so that everything about her seems more important and significant than anything else in the world? . . . Nothing more can be said than that these are human ways, and that every creature *likes* its own ways and takes to following them as a matter of course . . .'

Finally, we must mention another type of instinctive behaviour, i.e. instinctive 'know-how'. It is made up of a permanent chain of actions that are sometimes very complicated and always very specialised, and that seem to follow rigidly from one another. Such behaviour will occur in all members of a given species at certain periods of their life, and is directed towards ends that the animals themselves seem to be ignorant of. Actions of this type merit the classic dictum that 'instinct is an innate, specific, immutable, specialised and blind activity'. This is beautifully illustrated by Fabre's description of the nesting instinct of the sacred scarab beetle, which prepares a pill of cow dung for an egg it will never see hatch out.

Lest the reader be misled, we must stress that 1, these activities are very specialised, and occur in insects and certain vertebrates alone. Even here they are by no means the only activities in the life of the individual, and are generally characteristic of only the reproductive functions (pairing, mating, nestbuilding, etc.); and 2, the products of these stereotyped activities being 'marvels of nature', sometimes comparable to the products of human ingenuity (as for instance the honeycombs of bees), observers have been inclined to overestimate their importance, thus creating the myth of the radical opposition between 'Instinct' and 'Intelligence'. As we shall see, the opposition is not so much between instinct and intelligence, as

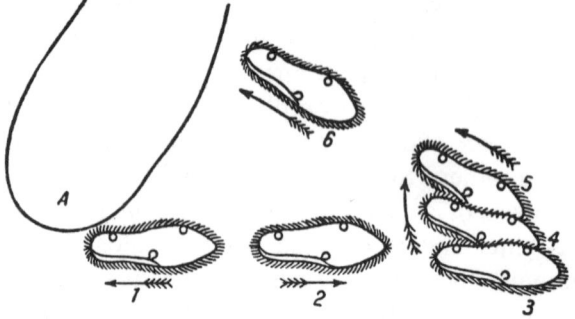

Fig. 1
Negative chemo-tropic reactions of Paramecium. A: drop of alkaline solution; 1, 2, 3, successive positions of the animal (after Jennings).

INTRODUCTION

between non-intelligent instinctive acts and intelligent acts, no matter whether the latter be instinctive or else due to the loftiest considerations.

Instinctive acts are not always performed smoothly. When obstacles arise, the unintelligent animal will attempt to remove them by trial and error. In other words, it will trust to luck until, quite fortuitously, it arrives at the desired goal. Thus the slipper animalcule (Paramecium) will swim about in all directions to avoid a drop of irritant, until it fortuitously enters regions where it is surrounded by pure water (Fig. 1). Another example, illustrating much more highly evolved behaviour: place a hungry chicken in a run closed on three sides, and let the bird see a heap of grain through the wire mesh. The bird will rush up and

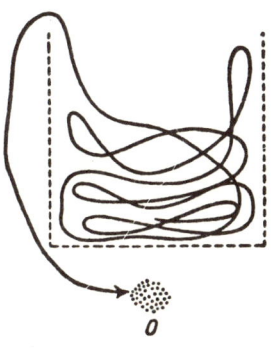

Fig. 2
Trial and error of a hen. O, goal object (heap of grains).

down inside the fence until chance guides it outside (Fig. 2).

Such stupid behaviour patterns occur right up the zoological ladder. Man himself, and young children in particular, fall back on these patterns whenever an intelligent solution eludes them, though generally they manage to learn from their past mistakes.

Let us now see what characterises *intelligent actions*. On the whole they differ from purely instinctive behaviour in that they are much more sensitive responses to external changes, unusual situations, and new conditions. The unintelligent animal, with its restricted number of innate or habitual responses, will go on and on trying to solve problems, until some accident comes to its assistance. A good example was the way in which our hungry hen 'overcame' its obstacle. The intelligent animal, on the other hand, after having tried to solve a problem unsuccessfully will spontaneously modify its conduct. In other words, it will invent new types of behaviour to fit new situations—it will behave intelligently.

We study intelligent behaviour by confronting animals—or men—with new situations, i.e. by posing original problems. W. Köhler, who is famous for his experimental work on the mentality of apes, and whom we shall quote frequently, has established the following criteria of intelligent behaviour:

INTRODUCTION

1. *Sudden discovery of the solution.* Intelligent animals discover their solutions suddenly, generally after several fruitless attempts. However, even their fruitless attempts are not usually the hit-and-miss affairs of unintelligent animals—the intelligent animal does not keep repeating its mistakes. In very simple cases the solution may be found immediately, after a brief inspection of the situation. Thus, if we place a hungry dog behind our chicken wire, it will sum up the situation at a glance and then race round the wire.[1]

2. *Generalisation of the solution.* A particular solution can be generalised for solving subsequent problems. For example, a monkey, once it has learned to use a stick for knocking down inaccessible bananas, will later be able to use planks, rods, shoes, etc.

Naturally, the degree to which a particular animal can generalise, depends on its powers of

---

[1]'Suddenness' is often a difficult criterion to apply. Rabaud mentions an observation on a magpie that he first made in 1904, and that he has subsequently repeated. A cat was holding a piece of meat in its claws. A magpie kept circling round the cat moving in on it all the time. Suddenly it pecked at the cat's tail; the cat turned, let go of the meat, whereupon the magpie pounced on the meat and flew off. The whole manoeuvre, says Rabaud, was apparently improvised right there and then, since it could not have been learned. The magpie apparently invented the solution. Yet all other magpies would do the same, so that it looks as if the bird acted instinctively. This is, in fact, Rabaud's conclusion when he says that the bird could not possibly predict the final result, and simply pecked at the cat's tail for the sake of pecking. Rabaud's hypothesis seems plausible, if unverified. Köhler's experiments with apes have the great merit of avoiding such interpretations.

abstraction. They are small with animals of little intelligence.

Every intelligent action is characterised by an *understanding* of the relations between the given elements and by the *invention* of an appropriate solution on the basis of that understanding.

To put it more simply: we say that an animal has acted intelligently when, confronted with a problem situation, it: 1, understands the situation; 2, invents a solution; 3, acts appropriately. This is roughly what Claparède means when he says that 'every complete act of intelligence involves three fundamental operations: posing the problem, inventing a hypothesis, checking its validity'.

These three fundamental operations are typical of all forms of intelligence. When the dog sees 'at a glance' how to round a fence, it has simply weighed up the spatial relations between itself, its food, and the shape of the barrier; at the same time it has invented a solution, i.e. it has realised what movements will lead it to the food, and finally it has checked the solution by finding out if it produces the desired results. A schoolboy, though on a different plane, will solve his geometry problems in fundamentally the same way: he must realise the nature of the problem, invent a possible solution by making assumptions, construct figures, etc., and finally verify his solution deductively, i.e. by showing how it follows from established axioms or theorems. The 'factors' of intelligent behaviour are more obvious in the case of the child than in the dog, since the child uses language instead of bodily movements.

The forms of intelligence

For long, philosophers and psychologists recognised no other form of intelligence than man's *logical and conceptual intelligence* based on language. Such intelligence may be briefly defined as the application of abstract and generalised ideas to specific things and events: adult man, faced with a problem situation, tries to solve it by using his conceptual knowledge, his principles, and methods which he has learned in the past. The forms of this type of intelligence have been studied by logicians since classical times, and their essential rules clearly established.

According to the older school of philosophers and psychologists, all other mental activities are purely instinctive. 'Animals do not think because they cannot speak', said Descartes, stressing, incidentally, the close connection between conceptual thought and language. 'Instinct and Reason', wrote Pascal, 'are as worlds apart', meaning that only man can reason, while animals got on as best they can by relying on instinct. No doubt, Pascal must have observed differences in animals' behaviour, and also their adaptability in face of new situations. Still, it could all be put down to training rather than to real insight. To use a more modern expression, the relative plasticity of animal behaviour was attributed to a faculty for acquiring conditioned reflexes and habits, i.e. to an associative memory.

Now, during the last fifty years, psychologists have learned to recognise forms of intelligence that are more primitive than the logical or conceptual, but nevertheless quite distinct from instinct. These types of intelligence can be found in higher animals, in young children and also in adults, and are known as *practical intelligence*.

Unlike logical and conceptual intelligence, practical intelligence is not the application of abstract notions to facts, but the intelligent use of movements and actions for dealing with the shape of objects and with external events. Dr. Charles Blondel has defined practical intelligence as follows (*Introduction à la Psychologie collective*, p. 194): 'It is the capacity of nearly all human beings to respond to sense stimuli with motor reactions, perfected not, as in the case of animals, by continuous trial and error, but by immediate concentration and the invocation of experience as a whole.' In simpler terms, we may say that practical intelligence includes all those qualities, ranging from manual skill and dexterity to the inventive ability of the craftsman, which Voltaire and the Encyclopaedists simply called the *Mechanical Instinct*.

The idea of practical intelligence was first put

INTRODUCTION

forward in Bergson's 'Creative Evolution', where, in a famous passage, he contrasted the intelligence of *Homo sapiens*, i.e. the rational intelligence of classical psychology and logic, with the creative intelligence of *Homo faber*, and where he showed that the latter must have appeared before the former: 'Intelligence in its initial form may be considered to be the ability to produce artificial objects, particularly tools, and to continue making them by a variety of methods. If we could ignore questions of pride, and if we would let ourselves be guided by history and prehistory alone, we should perhaps call ourselves, not *Homo sapiens*, but *Homo faber*.'

Bergson then pointed out that the first reliable sign of man's presence on Earth is the prehistoric flint tool, and that the chief stages of human progress are marked by technical discoveries, generally on the part of obscure craftsmen: the change from flaked stone to polished stone, to metals, to the combustion engine, to electricity, etc.

The notion of the practical intelligence of *Homo faber* has made great strides in contemporary philosophy. We need only refer to the work of Lévy-Bruhl ('The progress of the mind is due to the co-operation between the mind and the hand'), Edouard Le Roy's *Les Origines humaines et l'Evolution de l'Intelligence*, and Louis Weber's *Le Rhythme du Progres* which contrasts conceptual, verbal and collective thought with creative, technical and individual thought.

Modern psychologists, too, have paid much attention to this new concept, and are continuing to do so. Thus they have discovered and investigated the sensory-motor skills and practical intelligence of mammals and particularly of apes (Boutan, Köhler, Yerkes, Guillaume, Meyersohn, etc.) and the practical intelligence of the child (Boutan, Gottschaldt, and particularly, André Rey). On the other hand, little attention has been paid to the creative intelligence of adults. In short, the field of practical intelligence holds out great promise for all who care to venture upon it.

In the following chapters we shall study the main forms of intelligence under two sub-headings: 1, the 'lower' forms of practical intelligence common to man and animals alike, and, 2, the 'higher' forms of intelligence, characteristic of man alone, and involving organised concepts and the use of words or other symbols—i.e. conceptual, logical and rational intelligence. Language is the dividing line between specifically human ways of thought and those which are common to man and animals. In the course of this book we shall try to demonstrate the essential role that language has played in the evolution of the human mind.

Part One

PRACTICAL INTELLIGENCE

1

The Intelligence of Animals

We have divided practical intelligence into three types: that of animals, children and adults. All three are largely governed by the same laws but each has its own characteristics, since each is typical of a particular level of development.

Simple observations of domesticated animals leave us convinced that they have some measure of intelligence and this is also borne out by descriptions of wild life: beavers construct dams by whittling down logs and branches to just the right length, and manage to maintain a constant head of water by constructing a network of locks. Elephants, too, have been known to build dams to collect water for their bathing pools and, once captured, they can be taught a great number of skills (feeding logs into sawmills, stacking timber, etc.). The fox is proverbially sly and will pounce upon the hare in its form or the chicken in its coop, giving even the most carefully hidden snares a wide berth, or making off with the bait while leaving the trap unsprung.

Now, while there seems to be fairly conclusive evidence for the existence of intelligence in animals, only experimental psychology can distinguish between invention and real intelligence on the one hand, and instinct and conditioning on the other. Experimental psychology has shown that there is more than one level of animal intelligence, and that one must go far down the ladder of evolution before one meets a life-form totally incapable of inventing solutions to its problems. Thus even the hen is not completely witless and, so long as the obstacles are not too great, she will find her way to her dinner (see p. 15); in any case, her very manoeuvres before the fence show some slight glimmers of understanding. What makes her stupid is her persistence in fumbling attempts even when she is completely unsuccessful. Cats and dogs are far superior to her in this respect, and soon tire before insuperable obstacles.

Experimental psychology has also shown that the mental level of animals can be accurately determined by means of carefully chosen tests. The choice and scaling of these tests is decided experimentally, for experiment alone can reveal the difficulties of a particular problem. We must appreciate that psychology, in its present state at least, cannot make theoretical predictions as to what constitutes a simple and what a complicated test for any given animal or, when all is said and done, for a particular human being. The day every teacher realises this fact, children may no longer be forced into tackling problems that are

INTELLIGENCE OF ANIMALS

quite beyond them, no matter how simple they may seem to the adult mind.

In the course of his famous experimental work to evaluate the comparative intelligence of chimpanzees (Tenerife 1914-1920), the German psychologist Wolfgang Köhler confronted his animals with four types of problems:

(1) *Detour problems:* an obstacle is placed between the animal and its food, which the animal can only reach by going round the obstacle, or else the food is out of direct reach and must be hauled in by means of an attached string or other intermediate object (see Fig. 3).

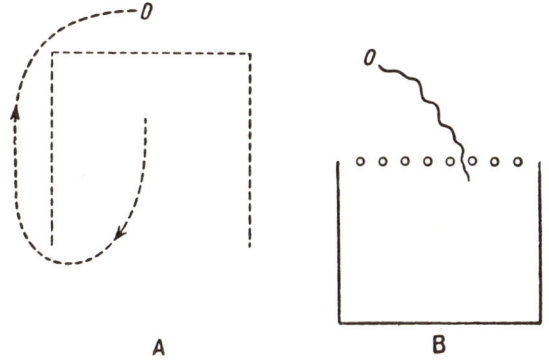

Fig. 3
Detour problems. A, roundabout locomotion. B, roundabout prehension (after Köhler).

(2) *Problems involving the removal of obstacles* (the converse of (1)): a box or some such object

is interposed between the animal and its food and must be pushed out of the way.

(3) *Problems involving the use of implements:* the food is placed outside the cage and sticks, planks, boxes, etc. are provided for hauling in the food or for knocking it down (Fig. 4). Problems of type (3) can be combined with type (1): a box, open on top and on one side, is put in position before the cage, the open side facing away. The food is inside the box and the animal is given a stick. The food must first be pushed out of the box and then pulled round it (Fig. 4B).

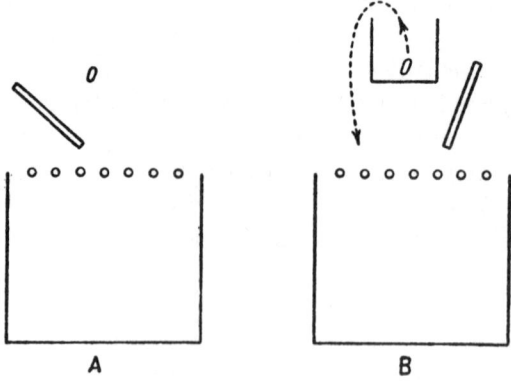

Fig. 4
Problems involving the use of implements. A, simple use of implement. B, detour with implement.

(4) *Problems involving the simple construction of implements* from components which, by themselves, are inadequate for coping with the situation.

INTELLIGENCE OF ANIMALS

The animal may have to pile up cases to erect a scaffolding, empty a heavy crate before pushing it underneath the objective, or fit bamboo rods into a long stick, etc.

Dogs and cats generally have little difficulty in solving roundabout locomotion problems, but fail when faced with prehension problems, i.e. they cannot haul in the goal object by pulling a string. While few apes have difficulty with detour problems, the lower apes cannot use a stick as an implement, and will haul it in the moment it has touched the food. It never occurs to them to use the stick as a rake, a little trick that is quickly mastered by the chimpanzee. Yet even chimpanzees are usually at a loss when it comes to fitting rods together, and only the most intelligent of them can solve problems of type (4). It is for this reason that psychologists have been so impressed with Köhler's best subjects (e.g. Sultan). The simple construction of implements marks the psychological transition from animal to man, and is as important a milestone in the evolution of intelligence as is archaeopteryx in palaeontology and ornythorhynchus (the duck-billed platypus) in zoology.

Other psychologists have invented complementary problems, some of which are extremely illuminating. Thus in 1934, Harlow and Settlage set up a problem for testing the intelligence of lower apes (rhesus monkeys). The monkeys had to choose between two or more strings, one of which was tied to the desired object. The problem was made increasingly difficult by crossing the strings, just a few such operations utterly confusing the animals (see Fig. 5).

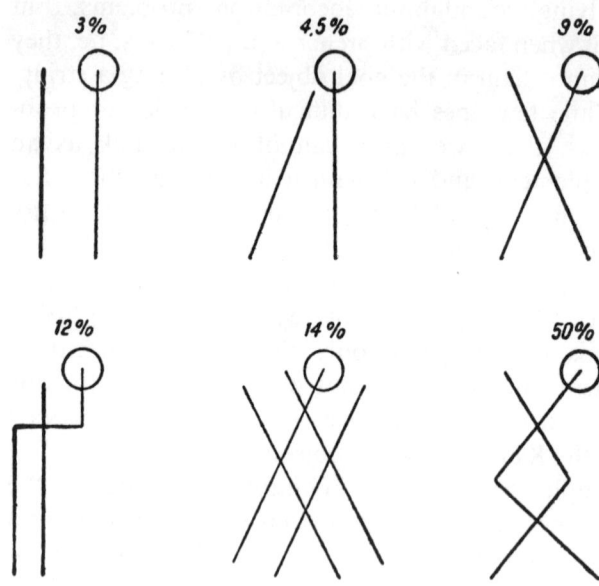

Fig. 5
Experiment by Hartlow and Settlage with rhesus monkeys. The figures give the percentage errors.

In 1927, Drescher and Trendelenburg made a spiral maze out of a roll of wire netting. The food was placed inside, and the animal left to make its way there, or else the problem was reversed. Cats

INTELLIGENCE OF ANIMALS

will keep walking round the netting and will not find the opening unless they happen to be facing the right way, but monkeys will get in, no matter which way they face. Having once gained entry, the cat will only get to the centre after many false starts and hesitations, and will be completely baffled when the situation is reversed, i.e. when the food is placed outside. The monkey, on the other hand, having explored the maze with care, has no difficulty in getting out, although that is far more complicated. On the way in, the movement is never away from the food, but on the way out the animal alternately approaches to, and recedes from, its objective as it winds its way through the turns of the spiral. This is an important point to which we shall come back.

In 1930, P. Guillaume and I. Meyersohn began their studies of the way in which monkeys use implements. For this purpose they designed a number of original tests, the most important of which are the set-square problem and a more complicated version of Köhler's famous 'diagonal string problem'. Köhler attached a string to a point at some distance from the cage, leaving the free end just outside the furthest bar (see Fig. 6). The food was tied to the string at a point which could not be reached from the cage under the given circumstances. The problem could only be solved by pushing one hand after the other through the bars and passing the string along until the food came within reaching distance, i.e. at right angles to the cage. Köhler considered the ability to solve this problem characteristic of anthropoid apes. In actual fact some lower apes (mangabeys,

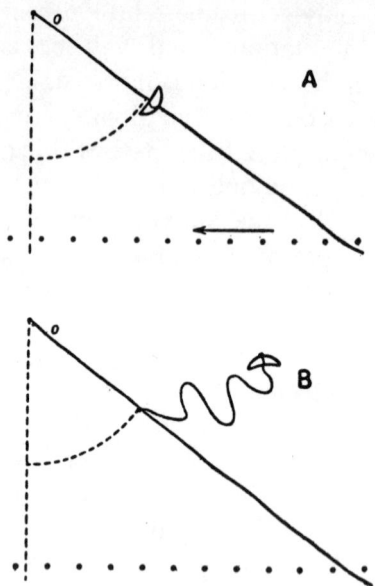

Fig. 6
A, diagonal string problem (Köhler). B, Diagonal-cum-auxiliary string problem (P. Guillaume and I. Meyersohn).

spider-monkeys, et al.) can do the trick as well, but only so long as the food keeps coming closer all the time. If instead the objective is attached to an auxiliary string (see Fig. 6B), the lower ape is completely at a loss what to do, while the chim-

A chimpanzee is shown building a 'house of cards' with a constructional toy designed for children. Innumerable experiments have been performed with apes since W. Kohler's famous series in Teneriffe during the first World War. Among the most remarkable are the 'token feeding' experiments of H. W. Nissen of the Yerkes Laboratory of Primate Biology. The apes are given 'coins' with which they may purchase food from automatic machines. They have found out for themselves how to save up for a substantial meal instead of spending their money directly it is given to them.

Above. An ant exploring a blind alley in T. C. Schneirla's ant-maze. *Below.* Plan of the complete maze; movable blocks enable the path to be varied. Ants learn by trial and error, but, according to D. W. Morley, research workers 'are convinced that some element of reasoning is present in ants' behaviour'.

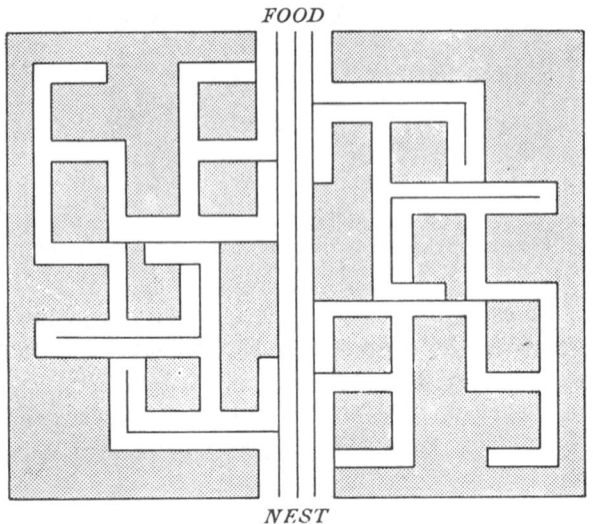

INTELLIGENCE OF ANIMALS

panzee realises that so long as he can bring the junction of the two strings nearer, he will be able to reach the food. In other words, unlike the lower apes, the chimpanzee will solve the problem in ways that do not necessarily involve bringing the object closer all the time.

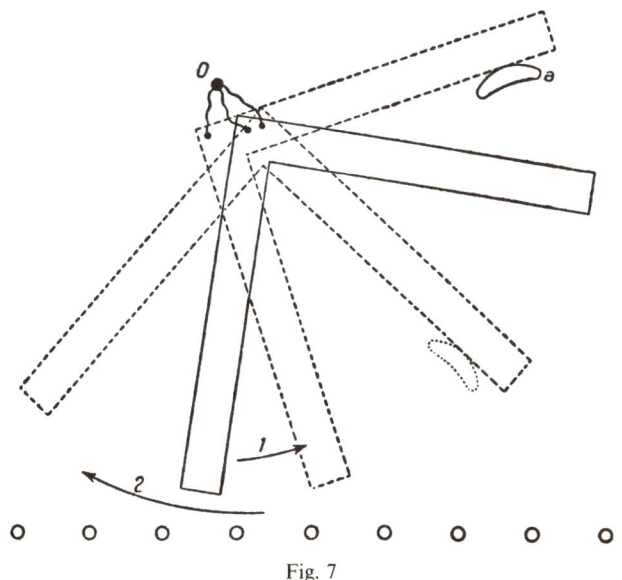

Fig. 7
Set square problem (after P. Guillaume and I. Meyersohn).

The set-square problem is a more complicated version of the 'tool-stick'. The set-square is tied to the bar by its vertex, and while the animal can reach one end, the food is attached to the other (see Fig. 7). An intelligent chimpanzee will have no difficulty in manipulating this new implement, even though the food moves at right angles to the animal's line of action.

These tests help psychologists not only to determine the level of a particular animal's insight, but also to understand the very nature of animal intelligence, and this is of greater value from a psychological point of view. Here then are some of the most important criteria of animal intelligence.

1. We have shown that every intelligent act is based on (*a*) understanding the relations between the elements of a given problem, and (*b*) inventing an appropriate solution. In animals both (*a*) and (*b*) are essentially intuitive procedures. The intelligent animal perceives the obstacles in its way and finds a solution by an *intuitive reorganisation of the perceptual field*. Thus the dog will solve locomotor detour problems at a glance, i.e. it will assess the spatial relationship between its own position, the obstacle, and the goal, and immediately solve the problem.

2. Since animal intelligence is based on the intuitive reorganisation of sense data, it involves the simultaneous presence within the field of perception of all the elements of the solution. In many cases 'optical contact' is essential. Köhler's monkeys knew perfectly well how to use a stick for knocking down bananas hung out of reach, but 'if the experimenter hides the stick so that the

animal cannot see it as it looks at the objective, or vice versa, so that looking at the stick directly the animal cannot see the objective, then, by and large, use of the implement is either prevented or impeded, even when the animal is familiar with it'. Thus even the most intelligent animals can only use such implements as are within their direct field of vision. Their intelligence is essentially object-bound. A man, placed in the same position as Köhler's chimpanzees, would behave differently and better; he would fetch a stick, a ladder, or some other implement and then return to the object, provided only that he wanted it badly enough. In other words man can reason abstractly.

All the same, even chimpanzees have been known to go in search of sticks, but only when they have learned to use them over long periods of time. As a general rule, monkeys have no organised memory to call upon; this being so their imagination is weak and restricted, or as Köhler puts it 'the time in which the chimpanzee lives is limited in past and future'. It lives more or less in the present and only bothers with what it can see before its nose.

3. Instinct and habit are most powerful allies to intelligent behaviour. Consequently the most difficult problems are those which run counter to instinct, or those in which instinct plays little part. While *instinct stimulates intelligent behaviour*, it may equally well act as a deterrent, for in man

and chimpanzee alike, the most profitable solutions are not always the most natural.

Today we can adduce a great deal of experimental proof in support of the foregoing conclusions. The very agility with which chimpanzees handle sticks is due to innate tendencies. According to P. Guillaume, a monkey will readily use sticks for the most different purposes: 'He uses it as a spoon when he dips it into water and then laps up the drops, as a fishing-rod when he dips it into an ant heap and pulls it out covered with its favourite insects, as a spade for digging up roots, as a lever for widening gaps between the bars of its cage from which it would dearly love to escape, as a pole for vaulting over ditches, as a shield against unpleasant or dangerous objects (fire, electrified plate, lizards, mice, etc.) as a means of aggression or practical joking, etc.' The lower apes, on the other hand, lack this innate tendency, and are incapable of using sticks as implements.

There is other evidence, as well, to show that instincts are of great help in solving problems. Bringing an objective closer is obviously more natural than pushing it away, hence problems of the type illustrated by Fig. 4B are extremely difficult to solve. Similarly, as we saw in the case of the wire-netting maze, it is much more natural to move continuously towards your goal, then to move away from it even momentarily.

INTELLIGENCE OF ANIMALS

From M. A. Urbain's interesting *Psychologie des animaux sauvages*, I quote two apparently contradictory facts: 'A jaguar was confronted with a so-called obstacle problem, based on the fact that all animals move directly towards their prey. The jaguar A was coaxed towards the bars B by some scraps of meat (see Fig. 8). Through

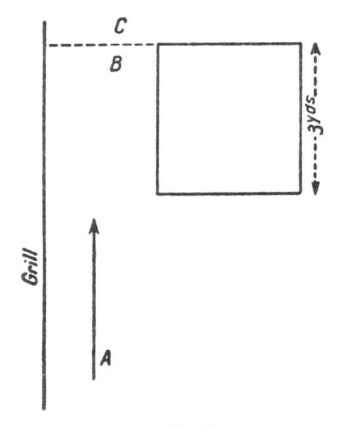

Fig. 8
Detour problem posed to a Jaguar
(after A. Urbain).

the bars the animal could see a large leg or shoulder of beef at C. The jaguar immediately hurled itself upon the bars, not dreaming of walking round the short obstacle. A bitch, in the same circumstances, would have hesitated for only a moment before racing round the obstacle to hurl herself upon the meat. The jaguar must first be taught to do so, and even then it takes at least ten attempts before it can learn its lesson. This simple example would lead one to suppose that the jaguar has a low order of mentality.' Yet one page earlier we read that 'gifted with fine eyesight and hearing, the jaguar hunts at nightfall, along the banks of streams and rivers. We can see it gliding along the water's edge on the look-out for birds and beasts. From time to time it stops to listen, carefully exploring the neighbourhood. Once it has discovered the prey it will approach it with patience and incredible circumspection. It creeps over the ground, makes detours to keep down wind until, when it has reached just the right distance, it leaps upon its victim . . .' Thus the self-same animal that is incapable of rounding an obstacle of only a few yards, will think nothing of making detours of tens or even hundreds of yards in its own habitat. While its instincts are of little use in the first instance, several impulses help and guide it all the way in the second.

4. An animal will at first respond intelligently by using its limbs or entire body, and only later will it be able to employ inert objects or implements. Only when the limbs—which are in fact a kind of natural implement—have proved inadequate for a particular task does the need for tools ever make itself felt. Thus the intelligent use of tools is a kind of prolongation of an instinctive or natural action, the instrument gradually taking the place of a given organ. Köhler has

INTELLIGENCE OF ANIMALS

noted that when a chimpanzee comes upon an inaccessible banana, it will first try to reach it by hand, then jump towards it, etc. The hand seems to follow the greedy eye, and the body to follow the hand. Only when these attempts prove abortive does the animal ever think of using a stick for knocking down the fruit.

Even so, the body continues to act as an integral part of the implement, the change from organ to tool taking place but slowly. This is shown clearly by Köhler's description of the way in which chimpanzees construct their scaffolding of boxes. He says that two problems are involved here: 1, raising the box, and 2, adding one box to another so that it balances. The one is not difficult for animals which know the use of boxes, the other is extremely difficult. The chimpanzees make up for the questionable equilibrium of their constructions by great gymnastic skill and bodily balance, and, by carefully applying their own weight (a problem in naive statics), they themselves become an integral part of their own construction. It must be said, however, that this physiological solution—using the word literally—is hardly a solution in our sense of the word. The solution of the problem only becomes entirely intelligent in the case of the child who, being a poor gymnast, is forced to solve the problem by adopting elementary notions of physics. In any event, we must remember that the chimpanzee always uses its body as a part of its own constructions, and that its substitution of implement for body is gradual and never total.

While categories 1 and 2 are characteristic of animal intelligence, categories 3 and 4 are characteristic of intelligent behaviour in general, and we shall meet them in children and adult humans. In all cases, however; instincts, i.e. unlearned patterns of behaviour, play a leading part in the genesis and development of intelligence.

2

The Practical Intelligence of the Child

The experimental investigation of the practical intelligence of anthropoid apes has usually been followed up by similar work on children, investigators using the same or similar methods. Comparative studies have proved most fruitful from the very start, and some psychologists have even reared children in the company of monkeys. Thus for nine months the Kellogs (1933) brought up their son with a female chimpanzee baby.

Now even before Köhler made his remarkable experiments with the higher apes, Boutan had carried out comparative studies of intelligent behaviour in apes and children (1914). He was the first to stress two important facts:

1. Speech is the strict dividing line between animals and men. According to Boutan 'children who have begun to talk act like little men, while those who have not, act like anthropoid apes. The difference in their actions seems to be unrelated to age, but closely linked with the presence or absence of linguistic accomplishments.'

We shall come back to the role of language in human behaviour and learn to appreciate its true worth and enormous importance. For the moment we must merely note that the one-year old child has reached just about the same stage of development as the full-grown anthropoid ape. The child is able to solve most of the problems with which the animal is normally faced, and is therefore said to be of 'chimpanzee-age' (Yerkes). But as soon as the child begins to use language, it makes rapid strides and fast outstrips the chimpanzee. Words and their relations become the transmitters of ideas and the guardians of memories. What the child cannot directly perceive it can now imagine with a consequent extension of its mental horizon.

This is borne out well by an interesting experiment devised by Gottschaldt. If a sweet is hidden in one of a number of boxes, set in a row, and if the position of the particular box is varied regularly so that, for example, it takes first, second and third place consecutively, the child who has not learned to speak will each time have to search through a number of boxes before it hits upon the right one. The same is true of even the most intelligent monkey. Both are evidently incapable of understanding the idea of a simple sequence. Yet the child who can speak will go straight to the correct box, language having enabled it to deduce regular connections between external facts from rudimentary notions of relation and order.

2. *The more intelligent an animal, or man, the less likely it is to solve problems by trial and error*

INTELLIGENCE OF THE CHILD 43

methods. Intelligence seems to cast an inhibitive spell on the free play of instinctive drives, and so to impede their expression.

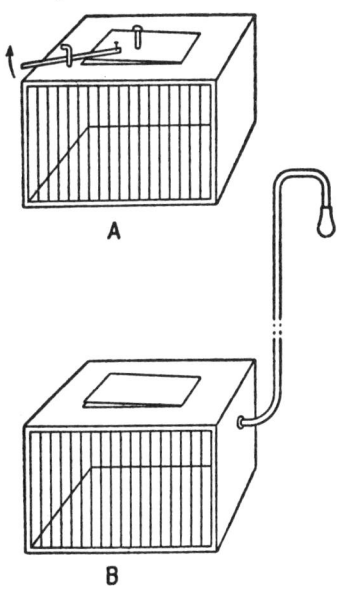

Fig. 9
Boutan's problems. A, box with clearly visible, simple opening mechanism. B, box with hidden opening mechanism.

One of Boutan's interesting experiments established this very clearly. He posed the following two problems to children and gibbons (comparatively unintelligent monkeys): (*a*) open a small cage containing sweets, by releasing a very obvious catch (Fig. 9A); (*b*) open a similar box by pressing on a bulb which releases a hidden opening mechanism (Fig. 9B). Boutan observed that the gibbons solved both problems in the same way, i.e. by trial and error, taking the same time to solve either, and that children of less than two years (and hence with limited command of language) behaved in exactly the same way. With older children the pattern changed: while they opened the first box at once, after just a simple glance, they rarely succeeded in opening the second box at all. Intelligent methods which are normally so superior, are a handicap in the face of problems that are not understood.

These preliminary experiments have illustrated two of the most important aspects of the child's practical intelligence, namely the great role played by speech, and the increasing disinclination to use trial and error methods.

Since the days of Köhler and Boutan, a great deal of further important work has been done on the comparative psychology of monkeys and children, much of it inspired by Köhler's experiments.

In 1935, Gottschaldt studied a group of one hundred hospitalised children between the ages of two and ten. He divided them into four groups in descending order of intelligence: normal, feeble-minded, imbecilic and idiotic, and set all of them the same, or nearly the same, problems that Köhler had set his chimpanzees. The results

INTELLIGENCE OF THE CHILD 45

were comparable and so was the order of difficulties which emerged. The simplest problems required the subject to haul in an object attached to a string; here the monkeys passed with honours, and so did all the children, except the idiots. Where the object had to be hauled in by means of, say, a stick to which it is not attached, monkeys, as we know, have greater difficulty in solving the problem. Both imbeciles and idiots failed utterly, even when the stick was placed in their hands and when they were actually shown how to use it. The feeble-minded could use the stick, but only when it was placed very close to the desired object; in this respect they were less competent than the more intelligent chimpanzees. The problem of assembling a long stick from smaller sections eluded the idiots, the imbeciles, and almost all of the feeble-minded children. Only normal children succeeded here, and, among these, only those of about ten years old. Finally, detour-cum-implement problems proved the most difficult of all, since they run counter to instinctive tendencies. Only half the normal children passed a test adapted by Gottschaldt from P. Guillaume and I. Meyersohn's work on monkeys (detour and implement to bridge a gap between two boxes).

Here we must mention Kellog's particularly striking hoe-experiment (1933) see Fig. 10. The subjects were a child of fifteen months and a chimpanzee of twelve and a half months, the two having reached approximately the same mental level. The experiment involved using a hoe for raking in a piece of apple which could be seen lying on the ground behind a wire screen, there being sufficient space for manoeuvring the hoe below the screen. When the apple was placed directly in front of the blade, both subjects managed to haul it in without difficulty, but when this was not the case they kept pulling in the hoe without realising the futility of their procedure. Only after a long series of trials and demonstrations (two hundred and sixty-five for the chimpanzee and three hundred and thirty-seven for the child, at the rate of ten a day) did the young subjects manage to solve a problem which seems simplicity itself to any adult!

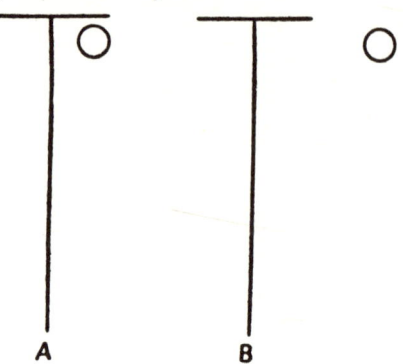

Fig. 10
Kellog's hoe experiment. A, solved after a single attempt. B, solved after approximately 300 attempts.

We shall conclude this rapid survey by describing some of the excellent work done by André Rey (*L'Intelligence pratique chez l'enfant*, 1935). His work deserves special mention not only because of its relevance to psychometry (where it provides a series of graded tests), but also because of its importance to general psychology, to which it has made an important contribution.

At Geneva, A. Rey subjected a number of children to a series of tests of the type invented by Köhler (e.g. the diagonal-string tests, which could not be solved by children less than five years old, and by only 75% of the five year olds) and also to special tests designed to assess their practical ability.

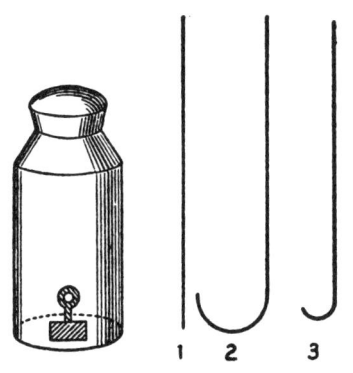

Fig. 11
André Rey's bottle problem. 1, Straight wire handed to the child. 2, excessively wide loop. 3, correct loop.

Here are three of these experiments:

1. To extricate an object from a bottle by means of a brass wire which must first be bent into a hook (Fig. 11). The problem is of the type that Köhler has called 'the making of implements', but in this case the implement has become a 'tool', in the sense in which we shall subsequently use that term.

Children of from three to five years old are incapable of solving the problem; they try to get at the object with their hands, used the wire unbent, or else twist it into useless shapes, even though, by means of models 2 and 3 they are shown what errors to avoid and how to go about doing it. Between the ages of five and five-and-a-half years, children are still incapable of solving this problem by themselves, though they will be more likely to take a hint. At about the age of six they can solve the difficulty independently, after a varying number of attempts.

Most children above the age of six-and-a-half years can solve the problem at once.

2. To balance a 'see-saw' weighted on one side, as shown in Fig. 12. There are four 'correct' solutions to this problem: remove the weight at B; balance it by an equal weight on the opposite side (at A); place a prop beneath the board at B; or pull the string at A and fasten it down by means of a weight. All the necessary materials are provided.

INTELLIGENCE OF THE CHILD

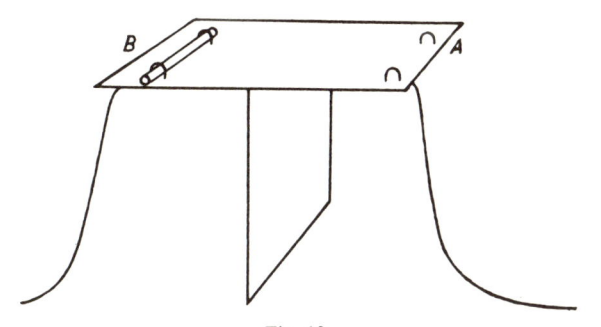

Fig. 12
André Rey's balancing problem.

Children from three to five years old, start off by *trying to balance the see-saw with their hands*. They seem unable to use the materials put out for them, or else they attempt absurd solutions—such as putting a support under the unweighted side of the board. Only the most intelligent arrive at some sort of imperfect solution such as piling up the materials round the bottom of the vertical support, and this solution is offered up to the age of six years. Between the ages of four-and-a-half to six-and-a-half years, one type of solution (the prop) is arrived at empirically, i.e. by trial and error, but from about the age of seven years onwards most children discover one of the correct solutions immediately.

3. To construct a bridge with two large and three smaller blocks of wood (Fig. 13). Only towards the age of five or six do trial and error methods yield a solution. At first the child will

50 INTELLIGENCE

hold one of the smaller blocks 'in the air' between the two larger ones, just as Köhler's chimpanzees will simply lift a case up to their objective before they ever think of sliding another one beneath it. Later the attempts become more constructive, but even so, they still involve the use of one hand as part of the bridge. 'At the most primitive level',

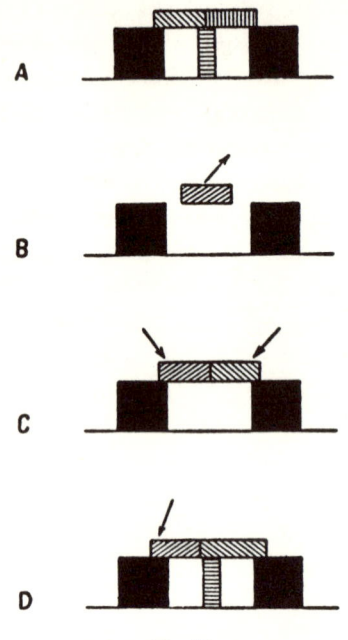

Fig. 13
André Rey's bridge-building problem. A, correct method. B, C, D, actual methods used by children. The arrows represent manual pressure.

said Rey, 'the child itself forms an organic part of its constructions, its hand being involved in the final structure; little by little this active involvement recedes before the discovery of the use of counterweights or props.'

A different type of experiment involves searching in a room for a hidden object. On a map, the investigator records all the subject's movements, obtaining an 'actogram'. A comparison of the actograms of adults and children (Fig. 14) is extremely interesting: the child makes random attempts, and, following successive impulses, its conduct shows no trace of system or organisation. 'Its itinerary', Rey remarks, 'is reminiscent of the

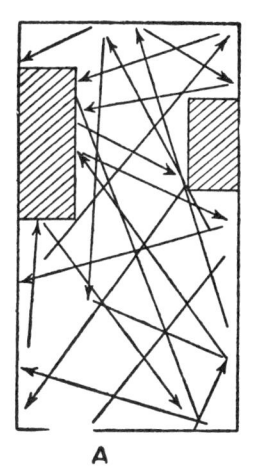

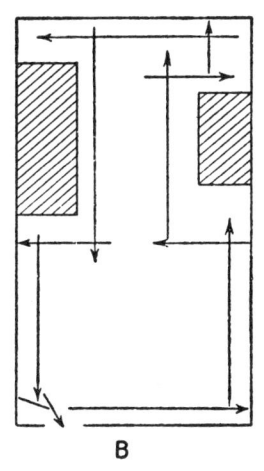

Fig. 14
Actogram of A, a child, B, an adult, in search of an object hidden in a room (after A. Rey).

movements of an amoeba in a drop of water.' In contrast to this, the adult proceeds methodically, from the nearest to the furthest corner, taking care to leave nothing unexplored. His conduct presupposes the existence of a plan, and the possibility of checking with such a plan after each failure—in other words the adult assumes a certain 'flexibility of thought'. The child lacks this flexibility, and in consequence it cannot systematically use its imagination to help with its activity. 'Here', says Rey, 'we touch upon one of the fundamental differences between the practical conduct of adult and child—once the child has adopted a course of action, it is incapable of revising it—its practical conduct is inflexible.'

Let us now sum up the main characteristics of the child's practical intelligence, as they emerge from the experiments we have just described.

1. At the lowest level, the child uses all its energies to tackle its objective directly. When it meets difficulties, its first reaction is to use its limbs; it balances with its hands, buttresses with its feet, pushes with its body, and so forth. These are organic, semi-instinctive reactions.

2. Little by little the child begins to substitute objects for its limbs, using a board as a support, a stick as a prop, a stone as a weight, etc. The objects have become implements, though, to begin with, they were no more than organic extensions of the child's hands. We have found a similar

development in the case of apes, but there is in

3. an aspect of practical intelligence which makes its appearance only in the child, the so-called 'mechanical intelligence'. From about the age of five years onwards, the child can solve certain practical problems in statics and dynamics. Thus its behaviour must be affected by some empirical acquaintance with the laws of physics, a kind of naive or intuitive science acquired in the course of its own actions and through its own efforts. In his *'Introduction à la Psychologie'* (1942), P. Guillaume expressed this fact very strikingly when he said that direct mechanical effects *on* the body are homogeneous with, and become adapted to, mechanical effects *in* the body (e.g. in the limbs). The internal forces balance the impressed forces, of which they are a replica and obey the same mechanical laws. An adroit child throwing a stone allows implicitly for the relationship between the weight and the trajectory, and when he pushes a swing he shows that he is familiar with its characteristic period of oscillation. Here, skill depends on a kind of intuitive knowledge of mechanics.

4. Language and conceptual thought endow the child's practical activity with a scope far greater than that of animals. The child can grasp situations that are far too complex for a monkey's mind, and can invent solutions that involve a variety of elements (as for example in the balancing and

bridge-building tests). However, this is only true for children of at least four years of age, who have already some grasp of language.

5. The practical intelligence of the child still lacks some of the characteristics of the adult's intelligence. In particular, the child is incapable of exerting methodical effort. It relies almost exclusively on trial and error, and reacts impulsively to first impressions. The child's abstract and conceptual thought is still weak and poorly adapted to action (we shall see why later on) and is more often apt to lead to absurd or fantastic conduct than to effective measures. The adult, on the other hand, proceeds by interrelated steps, and is more attentive, more adaptable, and more concerned with deriving the greatest possible advanatage from the given facts.

3

The Practical Intelligence of Adult Man

Experimental work on the intelligence of adult human beings is still in its infancy, but fortunately, in studies of man, reasoning based on observation may tentatively take the place of detailed experiment. The relevant observations are drawn from the work of anthropologists, ethnologists, archaeologists and historians.

Bergson has shown that man's practical intelligence is essentially characterised by the use of *tools*, and we shall now discuss the intelligent actions whereby man invents, constructs, and employs them.

What is a tool? An implement, to be sure, but not all implements are tools. Implements may generally be described as intermediaries between an agent and what he acts upon. We have seen that higher apes can learn to use simple instruments such as sticks and boxes, but that they are incapable of modifying them to any great extent. At best they 'prepare' them, to use Köhler's expression, as when they slip one rod of bamboo into another. Even so, their bamboo sticks, etc., are not tools in the real sense of the word.

A real tool is something more than the simple implement used by monkeys; it is an object so fashioned and adapted as to lend itself to the efficient performance of a given task. Examples are the knife, the axe, the spear and the spade. No doubt, our definition is a little rigid, for there are many gradations between the preparation of implements in Köhler's sense, and the construction of tools. Nevertheless, it is quite clear that apes simply prepare their implements—when they do—in order to solve immediate problems, while men use tools for tackling future contingencies, and construct them accordingly. This foresight is characteristic of man's practical intelligence.

Now certain tools are 'polyvalent', and merit special attention. The knife, for instance, can cut, pierce, slice, carve, and serve as a weapon; a piece of string can be used for attaching, binding and pulling; and fire, a kind of universal tool, has to be kindled and tended if it is to cook food, light our way, warm, burn, cut metal, temper steel, keep off wild animals, and, most important of all, drive engines. It is indeed the magic 'red flower' of Kipling's *Jungle Book*.

Very many of man's creations that we are not in the habit of calling tools, do in fact correspond to the definition that we have just given. Thus, according to technologists, the saucepan, the locomotive, the bridge, clothing, the yardstick, etc., are all tools, (cf. A. Leroi-Gourhan, *L'Homme et la Nature*, *Encyclopédie française*, Vol. *VII*). The reader will have gathered that a wide range of meaning attaches to the term 'tool'.

Now let us try to analyse the three main actions whose study constitutes 'the psychology of tool-making': 1) the invention, 2) the construction and 3) the use of tools. We shall only consider the simple and primitive tools which are the result of *Homo faber's* practical intelligence, and which seem to owe nothing to science or rational thought.

1. *The invention of tools.* The origins of the most general and simple tools are lost in prehistory. Nevertheless, the experimental study of the practical intelligence of apes and children allows us to guess at what really happened. Practical intelligence is, as we have seen, a natural extension of instinct. Now, we tend to seize objects with our hands, strike out with our fists, and scratch with our nails. Many simple tools are obviously fashioned for the express purpose of increasing the efficiency of these actions. This idea was put forward more than fifty years ago by Alfred Espinas in his *Les origines de la technologie*, where he formulated his theory of projection: 'Man instinctively projected the arm into the stick, the finger into the hook, and the fist into the club'. This theory fits in well with the facts observed by Köhler: 'The ape will first reach out towards the inaccessible object, before using the

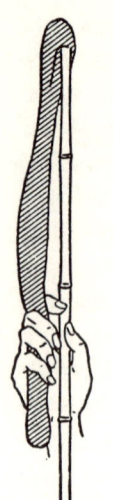

stick; the stick becomes an extension of its arm', and with Rey's findings: 'As children discover the use of implements, material objects gradually do the work of their limbs'. Thus Espinas seems to have hit the nail on the head.[1]

On the other hand, we may reasonably say, that his theory is incomplete. Obviously, practical intelligence cannot be the mere extension of instinctive behaviour, since the idea of modifying an instinctive action by introducing an external factor, must be complemented by some understanding of its physical and mechanical properties. Nowhere in the whole domain of practical intelligence is an intuitive or naive knowledge of physics more important than in the creation of tools. It finds its greatest fulfilment in man's handicrafts.

We may quote here several examples of primitive tools which still excite our

[1] According to G. Canguilhem (*Connaissance de la vie*, 1952, p. 153) Espinas derived this idea from Ernst Kapp's *Grundlinen einer Philosophie der Technik* 1877.

Fig. 15
Australian throwing-stick, or *wommera*, a three-foot baton ending in a collar made of bone or skin. It is grasped by three fingers of the hand and retained as the lance is thrown with great velocity.

admiration: the bow and arrow, the hook, the snare and the trap, the keel, the wheel, the Australian boomerang—which has perhaps been over-romanticised—and the so-called 'throwing-stick' or *wommera* which is used to hurl the Australian aborigine's very light lance with increased velocity (see Fig. 15) and is essentially a lever for extending the fore-arm as it throws the lance.

We may note in passing that the throwing stick is used independently by people who live in quite different parts of the world, and who have no ethnic ties, e.g. Australian aborigines and Eskimos. This tends to make us think that the same or similar tools were invented at quite different times and places (probably because the same psychological laws operate under the same natural conditions), a view held, among others, by the eminent archaeologist J. de Morgan (*L'Humanité Prehistorique*, 1937) and by A. Leroi-Gourhan, who says that 'the throwing-stick would appear to be an almost ubiquitous phenomenon, having been discovered in Europe, in America and in Australia, and dating from the Reindeer age until the Twentieth century' (*L'Homme et la Matière*, 1943, p.34).

The Middle Ages were particularly rich in inventive discoveries on the part of humble artisans, quite ignorant of the learned mechanics of an Archimedes or a Pappus. Lefebvre-Desnouettes attaches much importance to the inventions of the breast collar and the rudder, ingenious devices not known to antiquity, which played a large role in the social and economic changes of the time. Before then horses and oxen were harnessed by the neck, a very inefficient method since any increase in load would tend to strangle the animals. The ancients were consequently forced to use four horses for pulling one chariot. Thus the invention of the breast collar transformed travel and transport—one horse now doing the work of four—and may well have contributed to the emancipation of the slaves. The invention of the rudder did away with the swivelling oar, a difficult instrument to manoeuvre and to keep under control, especially in heavy seas. The rudder, with its tiller and hinges, considerably increased the pilot's power of navigation, and led to the development of bigger and better sails, which in their turn paved the way for the great maritime discoveries of the fifteenth and sixteenth centuries.

2. *The construction of tools.* The invention and construction of tools are usually simultaneous acts. Proceeding by trial and error, i.e. empirically, man invents as he constructs and constructs as he invents. It is only for purposes of convenience that we make a distinction here.

The construction of a tool always presupposes a) a purpose and a medium to be adapted, and b) the idea that there is some relation between the

INTELLIGENCE OF ADULT MAN

shape of the tool and that of the hand (or any other organ that will use the tool). For example, in making an axe we must bear in mind the eventual object of the tool (to split wood), the medium (the material of which it is made) and the relation between the axe and the hand (the axe-handle). In other words we must simultaneously take into account the medium on which we are working, the material with which we are working, and the organ that will eventually use the tool.

This is a complicated problem, whose immediate solution would require superhuman gifts. If the tool-maker nevertheless succeeds, it is because he keeps making corrections based on his practical results; a procedure which is, in fact, characteristic of practical intelligence.

By way of illustration, we shall give J. de Morgan's account of the construction of paleolithic tools (*op. cit.*, p. 150): 'If you strike the core of a flint obliquely with either a hammer or else with a piece of hard stone, you will detach a flake whose new face shows a swelling arising from a point just below the striking platform. This swelling is called the percussion bulb, and leaves a corresponding bulbar scar on the core. If, after having detached enough flakes from one side, you repeat the process on the other, you obtain edges with uneven, approximately zig-zag lines, which may be smoothed out by secondary retouches. Both types of edges are characteristic of the paleolithic age, the Chellean culture generally leaving an uneven, and the Acheulean an almost regular edge.'

In his *Gens de la Grande Terre* (1937, p. 55), M. Leenhard gives an account of the high degree of skill shown by the Kanakas of New Caledonia in constructing their jade-axes. The method of manufacture involves: 'the selection of hard unweathered rock; percussion with hard-wearing iron-and-chrome ore while the loose powder is constantly washed off by water thrown by hand; drilling with a torsion-string; abrasion against flat rocks, and polishing'.

Technologists classify tools according to their mechanical properties or effects. For example, an extremely large class of everyday tools is made for percussive purposes, and technologists distinguish between different types of percussion. Thus the axe, the pickaxe, and the cold chisel are perpendicular percussion instruments, since they are directed at right angles to the working surface; the adze, the scraper and the wood chisel being oblique percussion instruments. When the tool is such that the effort is transmitted to it by hand, either directly or by means of a handle, we say that the percussion is direct; if it is held in one hand, and struck by a hammer or mallet with the other, then the percussion is said to be indirect, and so the classification continues (cf. A. Leroi-Gourhan, op. cit.).

Such distinctions are of great interest to the psychologist, since they tell him what categories of means happened to be at man's disposal in the invention and construction of his tools. The number of such categories is, of course, restricted by mechanical considerations and also by psychological factors (generally the shape of the hand). The material of which the tool is made would seem to have less influence on its form than the final purpose. According to Leroi-Gourhan, 'the form of an instrument has at all times and in all climates been determined by the nature of the material which the tool will have to fashion, rather than by the material of which the tool itself is made. This is why the axes and adzes of prehistoric days had much the same shape as their modern steel counterparts'.

Be that as it may, there certainly are mechanical and physiological laws which govern the behaviour of the craftsman and determine the form of the tools he will construct. On this point, technology has perhaps much to learn from psychology.

3. *The Use of Tools*. The use of tools is just as much an act of intelligence as is their invention and construction, even when the particular tool has been invented or constructed by others. Quite apart from any technical skills in handling the tool, the very simplest use, the very act of copying someone else, involves intelligence. Imitation is far from being the mechanical act it is supposed

to be. The monkey does not in fact ape man. He cannot be shown how to use real tools (except by circus-training, a laborious method that is anything but imitation). The ape only imitates those of man's actions which he could in any case perform spontaneously.

As a general rule, if we are to use a tool properly, we must 'understand' it, i.e. understand the relation between its form and the task that is to be accomplished. This almost involves the ability to construct the tool; at least it requires a knowledge of the principles of its construction. The best workmen of the old school used to make their own tools.

The use of tools goes hand in hand with their preservation. Tools must be suitably protected for future occasions, since they are characteristically designed for long use.

Tools play a considerable part in the life of man. We are surrounded by tools, and they form a sort of artificial environment characteristic of man. 'What distinguishes man', says P. Guillaume (*Psychologie animale*), 'is not simply his diversity of objectives and his careful workmanship, but his ability to produce and preserve a host of permanent tools for a variety of purposes; he is inseparable from his arms, his tools and his fetishes'.

To round off our short survey of man's practical intelligence, let us note that though most of his

The ability of octopuses to learn and remember has been studied by J. Z. Young and B. B. Boycott. In the experiment shown here, an octopus which has already received one electric shock from the white plate changes colour and approaches the crab a second time with caution. Octopuses can learn to distinguish by sight between different-sized squares, white and black circles and other geometrical shapes.

This rat has been taught that food awaits it behind the panel showing a picture of two cats. Before attempting to get it the rat observes each panel with care, walking back and forth several times. It finally stops in front of the correct panel and, with its eyes pinned to the picture, leaps.

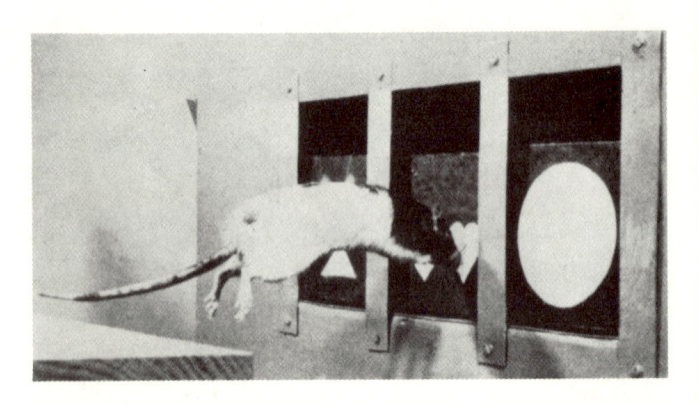

By varying the experiment it can be shown that what the rat recognizes is not the picture but the number *two*. Here, the number is represented by two hearts, and though they appear on a different panel the rat selects them after due inspection. Even when the pictures are replaced by simple black strokes the rat is still able to distinguish the panel showing two.

inventions are the work of skilled and intelligent individuals, society, language and theoretical thought have also played their part. It is only by a process of abstraction that we can separate *Homo*

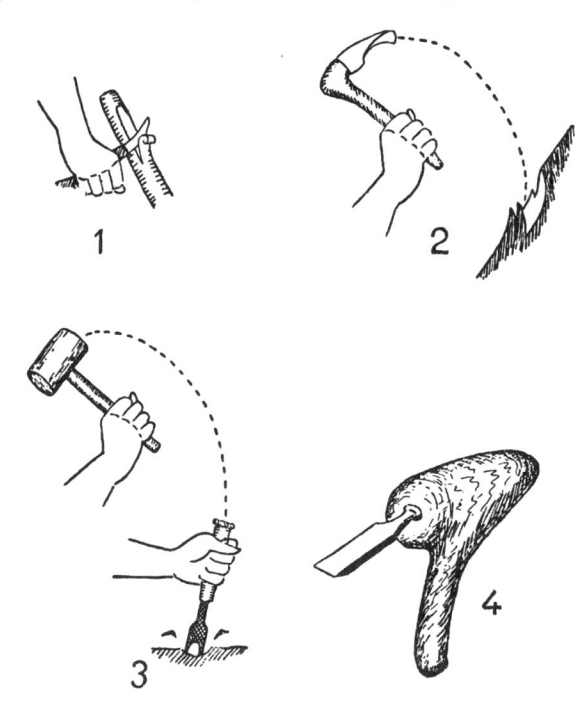

Fig. 16
Human percussion instruments. 1, Steady percussion (the knife). 2, intermittent percussion (the adze). 3, indirect percussion (hammer and chisel). 4, Adze manufactured by Eskimos and Lapps from a chisel provided by Europeans (after A. Leroi-Gourhan, *L'Homme et la Matiere*, 1943).

faber from *Homo sapiens* or *Homo socius*. All the same, such distinctions are unavoidable if we are to arrive at a correct analysis of human intelligence.

Since the above lines were written I have been able to consult A. Leroi-Gourhan: *L'Homme et la Matière* and *Milieu et Techniques*. These two works, based on extensive data in the field of comparative technology, are of great psychological interest. Here I shall merely mention two points he makes, both, I think, of great importance.

Leroi-Gourhan introduces the concept of *general tendencies*, i.e. tendencies which override the influence of a particular geographic and social environment on the invention and construction of tools. In ethnology, as in zoology, 'it is as though there were a predictable development from fish to amphibian to reptile to mammal to bird; or of an undifferentiated piece of flint to a polished wedge to a bronze knife to a steel sword. If I am not mistaken, these developments must reflect one aspect of life: the inevitable and limited choice which environment imposes upon living matter. Since it must choose between water and air, between swimming, creeping and running, the living being follows a limited number of evolutionary lines; it is because man has no option but to cut wood at a certain angle and with a given pressure that ethnologists can classify the shapes and handles of tools . . . *There are general tendencies*

INTELLIGENCE OF ADULT MAN

which give rise independently to identical techniques . . .' (*L'Homme et la Matière*, p. 14).

Leroi-Gourhan's classification of percussion tools hints at the difficulties in the path of tool-inventors. There are three distinct ways of applying percussion (see Fig. 16):

(*a*) *Steady percussion* is the steady application of the tool to the material and involves continuous muscular pressure (e.g. the knife).

(*b*) *Intermittent percussion* is the result of throwing the tool at the material while the hand does not release its hold on the tool. The arm and sometimes a handle which serves to extend it swing behind the tool, thus accelerating it and causing it to hit the point of application with great force (e.g. the adze and the axe).

Steady percussion is accurate and weak, intermittent percussion is inaccurate and powerful. Both types of percussion belong to the class of 'direct percussion'. In addition to the two types of direct percussion, there is

(*c*) *Indirect percussion* which combines the advantages of both; the tool is applied accurately to the chosen point, while the other hand holds another tool that is used for striking the first (e.g. the hammer and chisel).

'The third method (says Leroi-Gourhan) is one of the most remarkable achievements of technology; it has been used by very many peoples and no doubt it has been invented and re-invented down the ages; elementary though it might seem, its use is far from being universal.' The Lapps and the Eskimos, for example, do not use it. Moreover —and this is the important point—they are incapable of inventing it even when provided with all the necessary elements. 'When they are offered a wood-chisel (steady percussion), their first reaction is to take it out of its proper handle and to place the metal into a handle of their own making, inclined at 45°, thus turning it into an adze (intermittent percussion); although these people know the hammer, they do not use it with steady-percussion tools' (*op. cit.*, pp. 46-50). Similarly, Leenhardt (*op. cit.*, p. 56) has this to say about the Kanakas of New Caledonia and of the neighbouring islands (Uvea, etc.): 'The moment steel tools were introduced, the stone adze became obsolete. Its place was taken by the metal chisel suitably wired to the old handle.'

Such observations not only reveal the existence of several levels of mental development in *Homo faber*, but may even provide tests for establishing those levels. For man, the combination of steady and intermittent percussion tools is a difficult feat, just as it is difficult for a chimpanzee to join two bamboo sticks together. Some primitive men find these problems quite beyond them, and similarly, some chimpanzees will never learn to handle sticks.

Part Two

LOGICAL AND RATIONAL INTELLIGENCE

4

Conceptual Thought

The 'higher' forms of thought are the most complex, and involve organised concepts and the use of language or systems of symbols and signs (writing, mathematical signs, road signs). In other words they imply the existence of a social life, for although conceptual and verbal language are mental functions that are partly anchored in the anatomical and physiological structure of the human nervous system—no chimpanzee has ever been taught to talk—language is equally well a product of communal life. For these reasons the forms of intelligence that we are about to study are peculiar to men, and were last to appear in the evolution of the species.

We shall call these forms of intelligence 'logical' and 'rational', although for purposes of contrasting them with practical intelligence, the term 'speculative' might be more appropriate. The word 'speculative' is an excellent description of those special traits of human behaviour in which conceptual and logical thought come to the fore, i.e. the provisional suspension of action, the mental evaluation of the given situation, the invention of a rational solution. In contradistinction to practical intelligence, where mental action is directly bound to the given facts, 'speculative' intelligence arises in an abstract and imaginary world; here adaptations of ideas precede adaptations of movements.

The experimental study of thought and logical intelligence is in an embryonic state. We only have to look at Robert S. Woodworth's *Experimental Psychology* (1938), where a mere forty out of eight hundred pages are devoted to 'Thinking'. Still, important contributions to the subject can be found in Taine's *Intelligence* (1870), Binet's *Etude Experimental de L'Intelligence* (1903), Bourdon's *L'Intelligence* (1926) and in J. Piaget's recent *La Psychologie de L'Intelligence* (1947), which summarises his well-known findings based on countless observations of children. We shall come back to these observations later on.[1]

Most analyses of conceptual thought have been made by logicians. But logic is not synonymous with the psychology of logical intelligence, the former being a technique of manipulating thought, the latter a positive science concerned with actions and behaviour involving concepts and arguments, etc.

A knowledge of logical procedure is indispens-

---

[1] A good deal of the more recent experimental work may be found in Johnson's *Psychology of thought and judgement* and in Vinacke's *Thinking*. (*Translator's note*).

CONCEPTUAL THOUGHT 73

able for constructing a psychology of logical intelligence, since the two are related in just the same way as technology and practical intelligence. In fact, logical intelligence can be considered as a tool, whose elements—concepts, rational principles, methods, etc.—form a set of mental implements which man has had to invent and to perfect, and which he must learn to handle. Logic, which gives the rules of handling these implements, forms just as natural an introduction to the psychology of logical intelligence as the study of technology does to the understanding of the psychology of the tool-maker.

By analogy with the psychology of practical intelligence, we study the psychology of logical intelligence by investigating the invention, the construction, the development and the use of intellectual tools. At present we cannot even envisage the experimental study of all these questions. Nevertheless, logicians and epistemologists have told us a great deal about the structure and the evolution of rational thought. In the following chapters we shall examine what they, together with sociologists and child psychologists, have had to say on the subject of pre-logical mental activity, the better to appreciate the chief characteristics of logical thinking. We shall try to present this brief study as a continuation of the study of practical intelligence, and using the same biological perspective, we shall show how human behaviour is transformed by reason and conceptual thought.

Conceptual thought and language

Let us recall what we have learned about the intelligent behaviour of apes: when we say that an animal understands a situation, we mean that, in viewing the elements of that situation, it grasps perceptual relationships that allow it to find a solution. Now, apes understand difficulties and invent solutions in a purely intuitive way by the 'structural reorganisation of the perceptual field', to use the language of Gestalt psychology. Hence, in general, they must perceive the elements of the solution simultaneously.

Man's behaviour is quite different. He first 'poses the problem'—i.e., he analyses the given situation by means of abstract and generalised concepts, suggested by the external characteristics of objects. For example this *object* is *too high* to be *reached* (object, height, reach = three concepts). Thus he substitutes concepts for concrete data.

Then he solves the problem by reasoning. First he evokes relevant 'types of solutions' which he has stored up in his memory. For example, to reach an object that is out of reach, he must use a stick, throw a stone, climb a ladder, etc. Then he applies the best solution, i.e., he selects from many.

Thus, while the animal can only find a solution

CONCEPTUAL THOUGHT

by a careful examination of its present environment (in so to speak becoming part of it), man detaches himself momentarily from the given situation and finds his solution by reasoning. His reasoning is such that he can find possible solutions, even in the absence of objects which are an integral part of the solution itself. Thus reasoning is an intellectual act with far greater scope and efficiency than the intuitive operations that make up the practical intelligence of animals, and that are strictly bound to the perception of concrete objects.

Reasoning in man is due to conceptual thought, whose basic elements are *concepts*. What do we mean by that?

A concept is a generalised and abstract symbol; it is the sum of all our knowledge of a particular class of objects. Being abstract, it contains, or rather allows us to recall, the characteristic properties of the class of objects that it symbolises, and that distinguish that class from all others. For example, the concept 'dog' is the sum total of the properties that distinguish the dog from all other animals: it is a mammal, it barks, it runs quickly, it hunts, it guards sheep or houses—and so on. Being a symbol, it refers also to all members of a class, for example to all animals which answer to the description 'dog'. Thus, my concept 'dog' includes all that I know about dogs, my concept 'house', all that I know about houses, and so forth. In short a concept is a condensation of experience.

Clearly these properties of concepts depend upon the use of speech. It is only because of the word

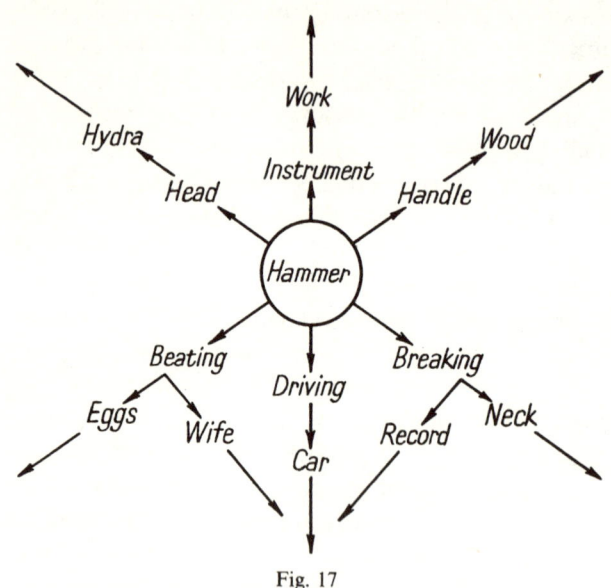

Fig. 17
A conceptual 'network' based on the concept 'Hammer': instrument for beating, breaking, driving nails, etc., with solid head at right angles to handle (Concise Oxford Dictionary).

that designates the concept, and because of the habitual verbal mechanisms into which the word enters, that the concept has crystallised out and that it can act as a permanent possibility of evoking a unique sector of experience.

CONCEPTUAL THOUGHT

Let us be more explicit. Suppose for the moment that we have as many words, A, B, C, D, etc., for describing iron, as that element has properties or possible uses. We could say, for instance, that A is heavy, that B is hard, that C is tough, that D is malleable, etc. Clearly, then, our idea of iron would be incoherent, and we should have some difficulty in evoking the malleability or weight of iron when thinking of its hardness or toughness. However, as matters actually stand, all these things are easily thought of, thanks to the single word *iron*, and thanks also to the way in which we habitually use it: iron is a metal that is hard, malleable, tough, etc. Thanks to linguistic symbols, concepts are systems of knowledge that are constantly within the reach of our thought (see Fig. 17).

Thus, quite apart from being a concentration of knowledge, concepts also enable us to summon this knowledge into consciousness whenever it is needed. They are, in effect, an empirical system of mental relations between a particular class of objects and all other classes. Logicians have emphasised this property of concepts by calling them 'systems of virtual judgments', i.e. possibilities in which the term that describes them is used either as subject or as predicate. Thus for logicians the concept *Man* is the sum total of all the judgments that can be made by using the term *Man: Man* is an animal, *Man* is gifted with reason, *Man* lives in society, the Greeks are *Men*, Socrates and Plato were *Men*, etc.

Clearly, then, logicians hold that concepts cannot exist in isolation—to think of one we must necessarily think of others.

We have only to leaf through a dictionary to be struck by this fact. We look for a definition of one word, and all we find are references to more words, which in their turn refer to other words still—so much so that we may have reviewed the entire field of human knowledge without having reached our object, i.e. the 'real' definition. To make up for this purely logical inconvenience, we have gained an enormous advantage, of particular importance to the psychologists; thanks to the interdependence of concepts, *our conceptual thought forms an immense network, each strand of which consists of a particular concept.*

Now, in a net, each mesh exists by virtue of the strings around it. The net forms a unit; rip out one of the strands and the whole net is distorted. Similarly with concepts: apart from their relations with concrete objects, they exist only in relation to one another. If we concentrate on one, we cannot help thinking of closely related concepts, and so on. Thus we can call to mind all our conceptual knowledge and, starting with the atom, we can conjure up the entire universe. In short, every concept can be said to have unlimited scope.

This, in outline, is the structure of conceptual

CONCEPTUAL THOUGHT

thought. Its elements—concepts—act first of all as labels for classifying the objects of our concrete experience according to their properties. Secondly, by means of the words which describe them, concepts are consolidated systems of knowledge; finally, and still with the help of language, they form a vast network containing all our knowledge. Conceptual thought is therefore a vast organisation of ideas which our verbal habits keep constantly at our beck and call.

The role of conceptual thought in human behaviour can easily be inferred from what we have just said about its structure.

It is the possession of so vast a network of ideas that gives man his superiority over the animals. Even the most intelligent of beasts have nothing comparable to offer. Animals cannot talk; they have no language for consolidating and organising concepts. At most they have an affective language for expressing emotions or intentions, and can grasp what psychologists call 'inferior abstractions', i.e. generic ideas arising from spontaneous processes of abstraction and generalisation. Thus Bergson pointed out that ruminants are bound to have a general idea of what is both 'green' and also 'good to eat'. But such abstractions, being general modes of action rather than forms of thought or symbols for classifying organised knowledge, are a long way from our concepts.

Even so, the chimpanzee seems to have general

ideas that are near enough to our concepts; for, as we have seen, the general idea 'instrument of the stick-type' helps him to reach objects that are out of his grasp. But then he seems to lack the ability to use this idea in the absence of a stick-object. These animals are more or less trapped in the present.

Man, on the other hand, can think up any concept by starting—theoretically, anyway—from any other concept, and certainly without having to rely on an actual object to remind him. He can think of real objects far removed in space and in time, can conjure up the future, the irrational, etc. The field of his activity is therefore considerably enlarged and his efficiency marvellously enhanced. Now we can appreciate Boutan's remark (see p. 41) that the difference between children who can talk and those who cannot, seems to be unrelated to age but closely linked with the presence or absence of linguistic ability.

Let us elaborate what we have just said. The whole of conceptual thought being constantly at the disposal of the individual, the sum total of his knowledge becomes a determining factor of his every reaction. Thus, in man, abstract thought always intervenes between environment and the needs of the organism. All human reactions depend both on external stimuli, and also on organised knowledge of objects and of oneself.

Moreover, this knowledge is largely of social

origin since the individual profits from the total experience of the particular group amongst whom he has been reared and educated. Auguste Comte said that humanity consists more of the dead than of the living. Similarly it is true to say that our thought contains more of other people than of ourselves.

Each of us confronts the difficulties of life armed with at least some part of the experience of his social group, acquired from his teachers or neighbours.

These remarks show how complex is our mind, and how difficult it is to study it experimentally. They also show that the real dividing line between man and animals, between the lower and higher types of action and intelligence, is the possession of conceptual thought and of speech.

Human memory and imagination

We have said that remembering the past and providing for the future are among the most important aspects of the human mind. We shall therefore look at them more closely.

The memory of animals consists of habits, which help the animal to act, but not to remember the past. While animals can recognise objects, people, and places, this recognition must not be thought to be memory in the human sense of the word.

Man, on the other hand, has a very strong

ability to memorise the past graphically. He can store, recall and identify, more or less at will, memories of a very great number of events that have made up his experience. He is able to repeat these memories, to others or to himself. Human memory is representative and corroborative.

A memory is a complex mental phenomenon. We are not always aware of this, and thus we often imagine, quite wrongly, that we can relive the scenes of the past as easily as we can see the present. True, there are times when the past seems to surge up in us spontaneously, but psychologists have shown that such cases are exceptional. Generally our memory reconstructs rather than resurrects the past. 'We remember our past', says Henri Poincaré, 'as we imagine our future'.

The reconstruction of the past is only possible because we have speech and conceptual thought, together with habits and social understanding.

In fact, we recall the past by word-associations. 'Words', said Bergson, 'are the carriers of memory'. Cross-examinations have shown that we remember above all what we ourselves have said or what we have been told. Human memory becomes organised, and can be used, by virtue of speech alone.

Bergson, in his famous article *L'Effort Intellectuel*, has gone to great lengths to describe the conscious and laborious recall of a memory. 'I tried', he says, 'to recall the name of a foreign author. It was on the tip of my tongue. I knew its form, its structure, and the feel of it. I tried to combine sundry syllables to obtain a similar name. But it was no good, the names I produced were always different from the name I wanted, without my being able to put my finger on the actual difference. Finally, after many attempts, it came to my mind that the name I sought was to be found in a certain book. So it was, and I was surprised to note that my very first idea had not been so far from the truth.'

Bergson uses the term *dynamic scheme* to refer to the original idea with which we try to reconstruct a memory. This idea may be vague, but it is very active in directing the search and limiting the field. We might compare it with a knot, from which invisible strands join the required memory to other memories. The more highly organised our total memory, the more cohesive its elements, and the greater the number of connecting ideas, the more easily a particular incident is recalled.

Thus there is a close connection between dynamic scheme and concept, both being systems of relationships between ideas and images—the mental attitude of those who argue about present difficulties without the aid of historical notions differs in orientation but not in character, from the attitude of those who pursue the 'Remembrance of Things Past'.

Moreover, in his *Les Cadres Sociaux de la memoire* (1925), M. Halbwachs has shown that the possibility of recording and recalling personal memories of past events depends on a sort of collective or impersonal memory incorporating all the social habits and all the abstract ideas about society that an individual has acquired in the course of his life. Experience shows that we are only likely to preserve and recall memories connected with socially important events or with recurring social activities, e.g. calendars, public events, etc. Briefly put, individual human memory exists only by virtue of the fact that social life drives man to reconstruct his past and provides him with the means for doing it. These reflections are in perfect agreement with what we have said about conceptual thought in general.

A brief study of man's imagination would lead us to similar ideas. Imagining means reconstructing what is not there, but what could easily happen now or in the future; the imagined situation being based on our knowledge of the past. Thus there is a strong connection between imagination and memory—the better the memory, the more reliable is the anticipation of the future.

Animals, too, seem to have a spontaneous ability to foresee future contingencies, but it does not go very far beyond the present. Köhler has noted how poorly developed this faculty is among his chimpanzees. We must not confuse intelligent foresight with animal foresight in storing up food—generally an instinctive reaction

CONCEPTUAL THOUGHT

involving no intelligence. Thus, chimpanzees will sometimes keep food in reserve, even if there is no need to do so, or else because they are inordinately fond of it. Then again, while they use sticks for various purposes, chimpanzees show an utter lack of foresight when it comes to looking after these implements.

In children, the development of the imagination goes hand in hand, especially at the beginning, with the development of speech. The child who does not speak has almost as little imagination as the chimpanzee, but the child who does, can imagine all sorts of possibilities suggested by the objects it sees.

This strict interconnection between imagination and language is confirmed by Head's observations of certain aphasics, people whose powers of speech are disturbed, and who have also lost the power of imagining, i.e. of mentally arranging, things in space. Thus while they can play straightforward billiard shots, they cannot play cannon shots, since to do so would require some imagination.

Even so, children show little foresight in comparison with adults. They are not interested in the future, and their imagination is almost entirely concentrated on games, and make-belief.

In adults there are various types of imagination, both normal and morbid. We shall ignore daydreams, hallucinations, deliria, depressions, etc.

which are outside our sphere of study and concentrate instead on co-ordinated or directed imagination, and on invention.

All normal forms of adult imagination are concerned with the future, and are conscious or volitional. The adult tries to meet the future halfway; he counts on the rhythmical return of the seasons; he knows that he must die, he is concerned about the destiny of mankind, and so on.

This is the reason why a great many of his interests are future-orientated, e.g. science, ('science, hence foresight, hence action', says Comte), technology, religion and magic (alleviation of suffering, warding off death), political activity (legislation), etc.

The general operations of the co-ordinated or directed imagination are extremely well described in Bergson's *L'Effort Intellectuel*, from which we have been quoting. Bergson has shown how, once a problem has to be met, man's inventive mind spontaneously finds a tentative solution, i.e. a vague idea of the general way in which the problem is to be tackled. This idea defines both the direction and the scope of the search for an answer, and is reminiscent of the dynamic scheme. Indeed, the mental attitudes of imagining and remembering are very similar, and when Bergson speaks of a simple scheme he means that it is not yet the clear and concrete picture of what has to be done, but a dynamic conception, i.e. a force

CONCEPTUAL THOUGHT

which directs thought and summons knowledge and memory to its assistance. The subsequent work of the intellect is precisely the selection and arrangement of those memories which can help with the solution.

Suppose an engineer wished to invent a bottle-washing machine. He might quickly think of a jet of water being squirted into the bottle—this is the dynamic scheme. Then he might quickly supplement his first idea by another: a revolving brush. Delving into his memory, our inventor will have little difficulty in thinking of a device for directing a jet of water as it turns a brush—such as a brush mounted on a vertical metal pipe through which a stream of water is squirted into the upturned bottle, while the pipe itself rotates about its axis, and so on.

This description of the intellectual operations of inventing is characteristic of invention in general (technical, artistic, scientific or philosophical). Just like the reconstruction of memories, invention involves conceptual thought, co-ordinated knowledge, and, finally language. In fact, the difference between the invention of a simple solution such as fetching a ladder and the invention of a bottle-washing machine, is only one of degree.

5

Logical and Rational Thought

Action and thought

We have seen that abstract or conceptual thought endows human actions with a range and efficiency far beyond that of even the most intelligent animals.

It would, however, be wrong to assume that conceptual thought has always helped action, and that it has always assured man's primogeniture. In reality, it has developed along a tortuous path, and this fact is of great psychological and philosophical importance.

It must be stressed that thought began as a social phenomenon, and that it served for communication before it was ever used for dealing with external objects. In other words, thought had an effect on man before it had an effect on things. We shall show that this contention is borne out by all we know of primitive man's psychology, and of his language. Primitive language is a special type of tool, designed to operate on man himself. The eminent linguist, A. Meillet, put it this way: 'If I should want an apple, and if I cannot or will not go to look for it myself, I must ask some kind or obliging person to go and get it for me. Language is indeed a marvellous instrument, for if we use it properly, we can make men move like so many puppets. Thus the simplest and probably the most primitive forms of speech are commands, ejaculations and exhortations (e.g. imperatives)'. This is also why Piaget, Guillaume and others say that the child, retracing some of the earlier steps of human evolution, will ask adults to do things it cannot do itself, and to solve problems that are beyond it. Language helps the child to turn adults into his tools, just as in prehistoric society, mental effects on men preceded mental effects on things.

Then again, thought derived its characteristics from man's experience of men, long before it derived them from man's experience of nature. The great error of past empiricists (Locke, Hume, Mill, Taine, etc.) was to think that man's mind was formed by contact with things, when in fact it was formed by society, by contact with human emotions and actions.

Sociologists (Durkheim, Lévy-Bruhl, etc.) have shown that primitive man projects upon nature ideas drawn from his experience of social events. Primitive society which is the savage's 'natural environment' organises the pattern of his thought.

According to Durkheim, primitive man classifies natural objects according to divisions of clan and kinship. The Australian aborigines, for instance, will tell you that the wind 'belongs' to one clan, the rain to another, and that a certain star 'is part of' a particular clan, as though it were a man. All nature is divided on the basis of social groups, and things appear to be akin, in the way that men are.

Furthermore, all primitive men explain natural phenomena by the action of supernatural forces, of superhuman wills, of mysterious powers, whose decisions are arbitrary and unpredictable, and whose methods of operation are unknown. As the ethnographer Codrington was the first to remark, these forces are the *mana* of the Melanesians, the *orenda* of the Iroquois, the *wakanda* of the Sioux, etc. Now *mana* happens also to be the sacred principle which ensures the cohesion of the clan, the sovereign force to which all its members feel subject. It is an emanation of the totem, of divinity, and of the supposed ancestor of the clan. (*Cf.* the works of Lévy-Bruhl).

These examples show how society and collective beliefs have given man his first systems for classifying and explaining natural phenomena. The first theoretical ideas, far from being reflections of reality, were the spontaneous projections on to nature of the social experiences of primitive man.

Similarly, the child will project on the world the daydreams of its 'egocentric' mentality (Piaget), dreams whose subject matter is supplied by subjective interpretations of experiences, etc.

RATIONAL THOUGHT

Between the ages of three and seven years, the child's mind is full of mystical and magical ideas, which closely resemble those of primitive peoples. Piaget uses the term 'egocentric' to imply that the child has not yet learned to distinguish between ideas about the world and ideas about itself, and that all nature is part of its feelings and intentions.

Moreover, the child endows objects with a will similar to its own: 'The sun *wants* to shine on us', it says, 'the clouds know where they are going'— and so forth.

Then again, the child still lacks the mainsprings of the adult's intellectual strength, i.e. that system of highly organised knowledge which we have called the 'network of conceptual thought'. Child psychologists, and particularly Stern and Piaget, have shown that childish thought is characteristically 'concrete, discontinuous, chaotic, badly-organised and inflexible'. The child's concepts, to use Stern's expression, are plural, i.e. they are symbols that correspond to a distinct number of concrete and specific ideas, and their interrelation does not depend on the hierarchy of notions that we have inherited from Greek philosophy, but depends instead on specific observations that are not necessarily inter-connected. Piaget has given us a particularly striking example of the 'chaotic' nature of childish thought: children between the ages of three and seven years have told him that small ships keep afloat because

they are light, and big ships because they are—
heavy. To the adult the contradiction is obvious,
but not so to the child, who uses two different
'experiences' of the same type for his 'explanation':
in the case of small ships, the water is stronger,
and holds them up; in the case of big ships, they
are strong enough to—hold themselves up. Piaget
also contrasts the 'inflexibility' of childish thought
with the flexibility of adult thought. We have
already stressed the importance of this fact when
we pointed out how the child's inflexible practical
conduct prevents its making a systematic search,
and profiting from past mistakes. The same is true
of the child's thought, for as Piaget has pointed
out, the child is unable to return to its mental
starting point, i.e. to reverse its conclusions
($A + B = C$, therefore $C = A + B$; all Greeks
are men, therefore some men are Greek, etc.).
Now it is this reversal alone which enables us to
make logical verifications, and hence to obtain
strictness and clarity. Lack of abstraction, discontinuity, poor organisation of concepts, irrever-
sibility of operations—all these characteristics
explain why the child is bogged down in contra-
dictions, and why it cannot adjust its ideas to
deal more successfully with objects. Even were
the child not given to fantasy, its mental equip-
ment would still be inadequate for overcoming
external difficulties.

We shall leave it at that, particularly since our

RATIONAL THOUGHT

conclusions are generally known today. We have produced sufficient evidence to show that thought did not arise as an adjunct to action and that it evolved in a roundabout way, passing first through the primitive or childish stage (social and individual rather than material effects) until it gradually acquired those qualities of logical organisation that are needed for dealing with external reality.

Some psychologists—Stern, Claparède and Piaget—have stressed the importance of this phenomenon, and given it the status of a law. Thought, they say, is always a stage beyond action, as actions and explanations involve quite different mental planes. The correctness of their contention can be demonstrated in several ways.

For a start, we all know how difficult it can be to explain our actions, and that there are a great many things that are far easier done than described. Conversely there are a great many people who can never do as they so glibly preach.

Now, at certain levels of mental and social development, action can be much more effective than thought. Thus, beautiful rock-paintings can be seen in the Altamira caves (Spain), though anthropologists tell us that the accomplished upper paleolithic artists who made them, must have had a very primitive mentality, and that the surprising perfection of their artistry cannot possibly be a true reflection of their 'civilisation'.

Lévy-Bruhl has laid special emphasis on this dichotomy between thought and action in primitive peoples. While their mysterious and prelogical explanations have no foundation in fact, they often act as we do, fishing and hunting with implements that are admirably designed and constructed. In his *Introduction à l'Etude de la Médicine experimentale*, Claude Bernard says that 'we can *do* more than we can think', thus showing that physiologists and physicians are also well aware of this psychological law. (Cf. also, Paul Lecène's interesting book *L'Evolution de la Chirurgie*).

Furthermore, thought may very well be developed for its own sake, without any reference to action. Thus oriental civilisations have excessively complicated certain forms of religious and poetic thought by rigid rituals, collective beliefs and subtle rules of 'good taste'. Examples are the Chinese civilisation with its mandarins, and the Byzantine religion in the Middle Ages. Such forms of thought strike us as being abnormal or childish, and so, generally speaking, do all forms of thought that arise out of indifference to reality or action—neurotic daydreams, for instance. One of the hallmarks of pathological thought is a lack of adaptability to external reality.

We should bear in mind, then, that rational thought which endeavours to understand reality and to act accordingly is above all a western form of thought, and, even here characteristic of only the normal adult.

Rational thought emerged after a long sojourn in the wilderness, during which action pursued its lone path in darkness. The two might easily have missed each other—the 'Greek miracle' might never have taken place. Considerations such as these go a long way towards depreciating the idea that man is 'a being endowed with reason'.

The rational mentality

Abstract or conceptual thought, expressed by means of verbal propositions or judgements, always appears in a more or less organised form. It is precisely this organisation which decides our approach to things and their relations. Kant realised this when, in studying the structure of rational and scientific thought, he was the first to draw attention to *a priori* judgements, i.e. those fundamental ideas with which the scientist looks at the world around him, and which allow him to carry out his experiments.

Though Kant was very perspicacious in his discussion of the structure of rational thought, he was wrong to think that the rational was the only type of human thought, and that it was part and parcel of man's nature.

We have just seen that, according to modern psychologists and sociologists, there exist types of thought with quite different structures, viz. the thought of primitive man, the child, the oriental adult and the western adult. Each of these types of thought has its own laws, basic assumptions, principles, and attitudes towards external objects. The different types are called 'mentalities'.

Neither the primitive nor the infantile mentality need take up much space in a work devoted to the study of intelligence, since the word 'intelligence' can only be applied to effective thinking, which is not characteristic of childish or primitive mentalities. Nonetheless, we shall state briefly what is known of these two types of mentality, if only to contrast them with the rational.

The primitive mentality has two main characteristics: it is made up of collective beliefs whose form and basis are determined by the organisation of society, i.e. the clan; it is a closed system in which phenomena are explained, not by physical causes, but by the action of supernatural forces. It has two directive principles, which are really one and the same thing since they express one and the same idea: 1, the 'law of participation', by which two beings are considered to be identical or to have the same nature if they are mystically tied to the same totem—e.g., a parrot and a man belonging to the parrot clan; this contradicts the logical law of identity, by which nothing can be anything but itself. 2, The 'law of mystical causality' whereby, for instance, the cause of an event, such as the death of a man,

RATIONAL THOUGHT

is explained to be the result not of sickness or a wound, but of the evil eye, or of some other spell. The magical tool of the primitive mentality is the fetish, a tool whose form and characteristics are derived from beliefs with no foundation in reality.

Piaget has shown that the infantile and the primitive mentality are very similar. Both are closed systems, for although the infantile mentality does not depend on ready-made collective beliefs, it is so highly egocentric that it prefers its own dream world to external reality. The child's thinking resembles that of the savage in that it, too, follows a law of participation which accepts supernatural relations, makes inferences without observations, and believes in a kind of mystical causality, viz. that its thoughts and will have a direct bearing on events. Hence we have forms of infantile magic, illustrated by Piaget's report that the child of a Swiss marksman was in the habit of arranging its father's discarded cigar-butts on the rifle-range, to ensure father's hitting the bull's eye.

Rational thought, on the other hand, can be characterised by two main features, that are the very opposites of a pre-logical mentality: strict logic and 'openness' to experience.

Strict logic means adherence to the law of identity and its corollaries, viz. non-contradiction and the law of the excluded middle: all other things being equal, any one thing cannot be what it is, and at the same time not be what it is. A is A, A is not non-A; between A and non-A there is no intermediate term. Because of this law, the concepts which make up the elements of our reasoning are as 'rigid' as the geometrical solids which mathematicians mentally transplant into Euclidian space.

Open-mindedness to experience is the mental ability to explain natural phenomena by natural phenomena alone. In other words, it excludes all supernatural causes such as the will or occult forces, so characteristic of primitives and infantile explanations. Associated with this experience-mindedness is that principle of determinism which governs all the acquisition of experimental knowledge, and which is variously expressed as: every effect has a cause, nothing springs from nothing, the same causes produce the same effects, all nature obeys laws, etc.

The two great laws of rational thought—identity and determinism—are interconnected, just as are the laws of participation and of mystical causality. They are linked less for logical than for pragmatic reasons. The civilised adult is alone in perceiving what he calls 'natural fact', and this conception guides all his thought and determines the laws of his mental organisation. This is something that cannot be stressed enough.

We say that natural facts are observable phenomena. No doubt this is the case, but we must

RATIONAL THOUGHT

realise that in so saying we have taken a philosophic stand, if only because we attribute two characteristics to all natural facts: 1, we speak of their 'objectivity'—natural facts are independent of us, they are what they are, and not what we wish them to be, and 2, we consider natural facts as the result of natural causes, as being 'manufactured' by nature. There is even a linguistic connection between the words 'fact' and 'manufactured'. Clearly, then, we consider nature as an aggregate of forces which transforms objects, organises complex structures out of their elements, or else destroys the complex structures to liberate the elements. This is obviously a philosophic approach.

The two essential elements of this view of nature, i.e. 'objectivity' and 'causality' can be logically distinguished, but are related in fact, since they arise together in human experience whence they are derived.

The problem of the origins and the evolution of reason has long occupied the attention of philosophers. All we can do here is to mention a plausible if incomplete solution, which has the great advantage of explaining the close connection between man's rational and constructive thought, and which accounts for the continuous evolution of intelligence. Its foremost exponent was Bergson.

According to his biological theory of reason, man is a living being, and living means acting.

Man is not an indifferent spectator of events, he is a natural participant. His thoughts are subordinated to his actions, and it is his actions that we must look at for the origins of his rational conceptions.

Man is also a tool-maker and a builder. At first he proceeded 'empirically', i.e. by constant trial and error. In this way he managed to create empirical techniques. Then he began to reflect about his methods of procedure. Little by little he realised that in order to make an axe, a house, or a table, certain materials with given properties were needed, that all results were produced by activity, that nothing evolved from nothing, etc. Then—much later, no doubt—reflecting on natural phenomena, he likened them to the products of his industry, considering them as 'facts' i.e. the products of natural activity. Thus he extended the ideas derived from his work to nature at large, and began to realise that nature too, produces nothing from nothing and that everything is determined. For a long time, he even had the wrong belief that nature did nothing without intent. Thus, as Bergson put it in his famous phrase, *Homo faber* was transformed into *Homo sapiens*.

No doubt, social causes have played a large part in this transformation. Nevertheless, their role could not have been predominant, or western adult reason could never have emerged from the absurdities of a pre-logical mentality. Far from being the extension of that mentality, reason constitutes its direct opposite. The efficiency of rational thought in the physical world can only be due to the fact that reason was formed by contact with physical reality.

The empirical and the rational

Man's purely constructive activity proceeds, as we have seen, by methodical trial and error. We call this an empirical form of activity.

Hand in hand with the introduction of rational thought into techniques went new modes of behaviour. Man's activity became methodical and rational. From now on he could go straight towards his goal without having to grope in the dark. Now he could use reason to decide what he wanted and how to go about getting it. He constructed more and more complicated implements, such as wheels, levers, vices, etc.—and finally, machines of all kinds. Then he began to look into nature itself, the better to harness her to his purpose.

It is not our intention to give a detailed description of the methods used for carrying out this rational activity; that is the task of logic. Here we shall merely note some points that are needed for a psychological definition. In their study of the structure of scientific thought, logicians have shown that all rational investigations are made up of analysis and synthesis, and that the investigator has to proceed in two opposite directions; in splitting up his data, he must first discover the elements or simple constituent factors, which he must then re-combine for explaining natural laws. Analysis, using the word in its most general sense, is always a method of discovering elements, laws or principles; synthesis is sometimes a method of verifying the results of the analysis, and sometimes a method of explaining the given facts in a new way. To reach understanding, we must always discover the simple by examining the complex, and then reconstruct the complex by starting from the simple.

It is this form of intelligence that Bergson had in mind when he said that intelligence is characterised by the systematic breaking down of data, followed by their systematic reconstruction. Compare this definition with his 'intelligence . . . is the capacity to construct artificial objects; in particular, tools'. These definitions clearly illustrate Bergson's distinction between rational and practical intelligence.

Here we must draw the reader's attention to an important point: logicians have shown that there is a close connection between the intelligibility of rational ideas and their constructive value. This connection becomes particularly obvious when we make practical comparisons between rational and empirical procedures. Such comparisons also

RATIONAL THOUGHT

demonstrate how much more reliable and efficient rational solutions are.

Two concrete and very simple mathematical examples will suffice to illustrate this point. Let us suppose that we must halve the apple harvest of an orchard between two partners. This can be done in two ways. We can simply make two heaps that are apparently equal. Now if one of the partners is suspicious, he will always feel that he has been cheated and there is no way of convincing him of the contrary. The second method is to make two heaps, picking out one apple at a time. In that case there can be no suspicions, provided the apples are all of one kind. The first method is empirical, and uncertain. The second is rational, the result being the rational consequence of the actions leading up to it. We are, in fact, quite sure that the two piles are equal, because we have repeated the same number of operations for each one. This is the dawn of arithmetic; number is the quantity that is formed by adding unity to itself; two numbers are equal if they are constructed by the addition of the same number of unities.

Another example. Let us suppose that we wish to construct a round disc. Again there are two ways in which we can do this, or rather two types of ways: one is to snip off the corners of a square, then the new corners, etc. This procedure is uncertain and slow; it is empirical. The other method is to take any point on the square, to mark off equidistant points all round it, to join these points and to cut the material along the line thus obtained. This is the rational method. The smoothness of the curve depends, in a perfectly clear and intelligible way, on the elements and movements by which it has been constructed. Moreover, we have constructed one of the fundamental notions of geometry, the circumference of the circle, or the locus of a point moving at an equal distance from a fixed point.

Here we have seen what a rational action really is: it is an action whose results depend quite manifestly on the elements that have gone into its making. Similarly, a rational idea is an idea that we construct in our minds, in a way that follows step by step from the elements. The act of thinking by which we grasp the possibility of such constructions is called 'rational intuition'.

The basic ideas of mathematics are the results of rational intuitions, and provide us with methods for the rational construction of mathematical objects. Considered in relation to action and to reality, the idea of a circle is nothing but the ideal way of constructing a real form.

We have no knowledge how these basic mathematical ideas were discovered, but we do know that some Pacific tribes still divide their cocoa harvest into heaps, because they cannot count above ten. As regards the origin of such geometric ideas as the circle, we may reasonably suppose that discs, wheels, rounded pots, etc., were constructed empirically until some dissatisfied bright spark hit upon the happy idea that all circles have centres, and that all points on the circumference are equidistant from it. In any event, we have archaeological evidence to show that pots were rounded by hand long before they were thrown on the wheel.

In conclusion, we must stress the fact that mathematical thinking was responsible for the introduction of mass production into technology, mass production involving an exact definition of individual operations and the ability to predict their results. This is the essential part played by mathematics in modern industry. The first mathematical discoveries gave humanity so tremendous an impetus that they were credited with divine attributes: 'God', said the Greeks, 'is a great geometrician'.

The systematic solution of problems

Now we must discuss the solution of complex problems by rational methods, and illustrate the chief characteristics of the most highly-evolved forms of intelligent behaviour. Once again we shall draw on mathematical examples, because of their exceptional lucidity.

Logicians have pointed out that mathematicians conduct their arguments by analysis and synthesis. We have already defined these terms as they are generally used; now we must see how mathematicians use them.

Analysis is a method of resolving problems; in Greek, *ana*—means 'back', and *lysis* means freeing, i.e. resolution. And in fact, we have seen that analysis is the reduction of results to the original elements. We begin by assuming a truth, a fact or a relation, and going back step by step, we finally arrive at truths that are known intuitively or through established theorems.

Mathematical synthesis is the method used for demonstrating analytical principles. 'Synthesis' is another Greek word, signifying the action of putting together. It consists in effect of putting together principles, like so many bricks, and then using them for the logical construction of the required truth. Thus, unlike analysis, synthesis is not a method of solving problems, but a method of proof or demonstration. It gives an overall view of the deduction, and consolidates the evidence in its favour.

Here we shall deal with analysis alone, since we are more interested in the methodical solution of problems. We shall try to illustrate the procedure and the scope of this method by an elementary geometrical problem.

Given a concave quadrilateral ABCD, compare the re-entrant angle C with the sum of the three other angles, A, B, D—i.e., find out whether the sum of their angles is larger or smaller than, or

RATIONAL THOUGHT

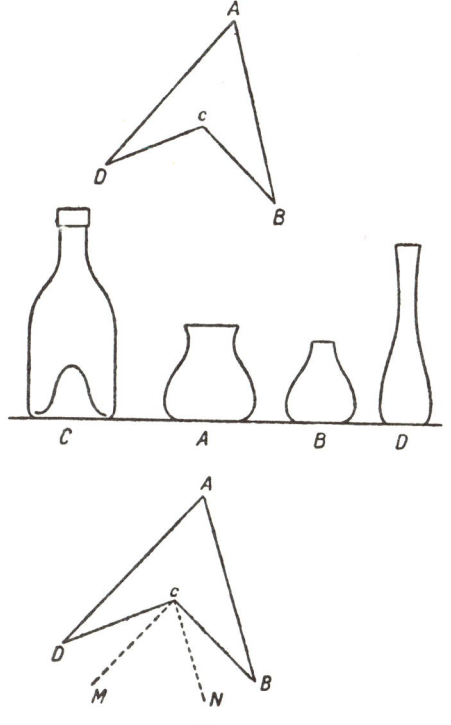

107

Fig. 18
Solution of a geometry problem.

equal to, C. (Fig. 18). Let us proceed analytically. Suppose that C is greater than the sum of A, B and D; i.e. that C contains at least these three angles (the immediate condition). The problem then is to transfer the angles A, B, and D into the angle C (second condition). How are we to achieve this?

If we could proceed experimentally we could use a protractor to draw the angles A, B, and D inside C. We would be doing the same thing if, in order to compare the capacity of flask C with flasks A, B, and D, we were to fill A, B, and D with water and empty them into C. But geometry is a logical and not an experimental science; its operations must all be so precise that they can be verified by previously established propositions. Thus, it is by geometric methods that we must transport the angles A, B and D into C (third condition). Now anyone with even the slightest knowledge of geometry carries a host of appropriate methods in his head. He could, for instance, construct parallel lines through C, making CM parallel to AD and CN parallel to AB. ∠DCM = ∠D (alternate), ∠MCN = ∠A (corresponding) and ∠NCB = ∠B (alternate). Hence ∠C is completely equal to ∠'s A, B, and D. The problem is solved.

By and large then, the analytical method is the transformation of the problem by substituting a series of simpler problems that will lead to the solution. This method is a *sine qua non* of all mathematical progress, and those who can use it have what is called a mathematical knack. Nine-tenths of all pupils are incapable of solving mathematical problems by analysis. All they can do is to repeat mechanically the synthetic proofs they have been taught and these are quite useless for an original solution of problems. Whenever they are in difficulties, they leaf hurriedly through their geometry books hoping that they might hit upon a theorem which might lead them to the proof, or else they copy solutions from similar problems. But the simplest type of new problem baffles them completely, even though Plato and Pappus of Alexandria were familiar with the analytical method more than two thousand years ago! This is what Descartes had to say: 'Those who do not use the analytical method are like a man who goes on a treasure hunt and spends his days running about the countryside in the hope that some passer-by might have dropped some treasure'. In the language of present-day psychology, the only alternative to methodical geometric analysis is the primitive and unintelligent 'method' of trial and error, a method on which all of us—men and animals alike—fall back whenever we find that we have completely lost our grip on a problem.

The Greek method of analysis is complemented by Descartes' four rules, put forward in his *Discourse de la Methode*. The first is the rule of evidence, a general admonition to intellectual wisdom ('Believe only in what is absolutely certain', etc.). Rules 2 and 3 state more or less, the following: 'Break down the difficulties into as many smaller problems as may be needed for their solution; in other words, analyse complex questions by attacking their elements successively;

always proceed by degrees from the simple to the more complicated, and assume that there must be a connection between them, even if, to begin with, you are unable to see it. Your knowledge of simple facts will then lead you quite naturally to an understanding of the more complex facts'.

Here is a problem (Fig. 19), the solution of which involves using the first three rules: given a billiard-cue and two balls, construct the path of one ball if it must hit all four cushions before colliding with the other ball. (Note that if the first ball is to obey the law of reflection it must not be spun on its vertical axis).

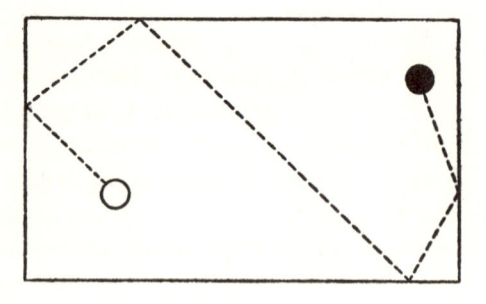

Fig. 19
Billiard problem.

We leave the reader to solve this problem, which needs only the most elementary knowledge of geometry, but cannot be solved unless the difficulties are 'broken down', i.e. unless the problem is resolved into a set of simpler problems. This can be done by considering what happens to the ball when it has to hit one wall only (instead of four), and then proceeding by steps to the final solution. Of course, these steps are increasingly complicated, as we consider first reflection from one wall, then two walls, etc.

The fourth rule of Descartes: 'Make sure you have not omitted any relevant factors' is an integral part of all inventive procedures. More precisely, it corresponds to the second of three essential operations: 1, Pose the problem with maximum clarity; 2, Remember and review all the possible solutions or combinations of elements; 3, Decide which of these is the best and carefully scrutinise your choice.

All studies of inventive procedures have, in fact, shown that inventors generally obey these rules. Those interested are referred to Claparède's and Hadamard's remarks in the symposium published in 1937 by the Centre International de Synthèse 'L'Invention'.[1]

If now we ask ourselves what are the similarities and what the differences between the way in which man solves his everyday practical problems (such as: 'this object is too high to reach; let's get a ladder') and the rational methods needed for solving theoretical (e.g. mathematical) problems of a more or less complicated nature, we come to the following conclusions. First, in every case,

[1] *Cf.* Taton: *Reason and Chance in Scientific Discovery* (Hutchinson).

after having 'posed the problem', i.e. substituted abstract ideas for concrete data, and after having grasped the relations between these ideas, he consults his memory to choose the best of all the possible solutions. Second, in the case of complicated, e.g. mathematical problems, he breaks them down into a series of subsidiary problems and continues the process until he can find a solution by immediate reference to experience. Third, he uses the simple, specific or partial solutions discovered analytically for returning, step by step, to the complicated problem.

Briefly, then, the general characteristics of the rational method are the correct substitution of lesser and resolvable difficulties for insuperable obstacles. In effect, the method is a kind of detour procedure.

There is nothing surprising in such procedures. We use them spontaneously in practice; when we cannot break a bundle of sticks, we undo the bundle and break up the sticks one by one. The really new thing in solving mathematical problems is not the general thought-process, but the special way in which it operates: mathematical operations being rational rather than empirical.

Our mental operations are originally spontaneous and subconscious. The aim of logic is to select the most effective, to perfect them, and to make them conscious. In other words, logic is nothing but the totality of rules, derived from the study of the spontaneous operations of thought, for raising these operations to their maximum efficiency.

CONCLUSION

We have sketched the evolution of intelligence from its lowest to its highest forms. We saw how animal intelligence detached itself from instinct, how implements gradually took the place of limbs, and how trial and error gave way to the invention of rational solutions. We discussed the development of thought and speech in the child, and stressed the tremendous new possibilities of action. This new stage was marked also by the acquisition of a 'naïve physics', so indispensible for the progress of practical intelligence.

We saw that, historically, the intelligence of adult man developed along two distinct lines: first action and then thought. Active intelligence in man first developed as the practical intelligence of *Homo faber*, characterised by the production and use of increasingly perfected tools. These tools were the rewards for much patience and careful observation, and the results of continuous improvements based on past experience and an intuitive trust in naïve physics. In this way early man obtained results which still astonish us today. Finally, after having first strayed into the *cul-de-sac* of the 'primitive mentality', conceptual intelligence grew into the logical and rational

CONCLUSION 115

intelligence of *Homo sapiens* with its extraordinarily efficient set of mental tools—the continuous network of abstract thought, logical rules and rational methods. As action became less and less empirical, greater stress was placed upon accurate production of results, sureness and swiftness of execution, and mass production. It is this, the highest type of intelligence, towards which all the efforts of Western civilisation have been directed ever since the days of the first Greek geometricians.

While the evolution of intelligence proceeded by definite stages, in retrospect it appears to be an unbroken line starting with the transition from purely instinctive reactions, followed by the gradual extension of limbs by tools, the substitution of directed and organised effort for trial and error, and finally the fusion of rational and empirical procedures. A thin strand connects the Paramecium, which swims about wildly to avoid a drop of irritant, the chicken which rushes madly in front of the wire netting that separates it from its food, and the child who will search for an object without any plan, with the adult who may begin by trial and error, but who profits from his mistakes. Similarly, there is a close connection between the sticks of the lower apes, the bamboo poles of chimpanzees, the 'fishing' hooks of children, the hammer-stones, stone axes, and knives of primitive man, and such tools as are used by the modern craftsman. This continuity is due to the fact that, by and large, intelligence evolved under the aegis of practical activity which, governed as it is by physiological and physical laws, can change but slowly.

However, there is also a discontinuous aspect of the evolution of intelligence which is due to the fact that all changes in form produce new characteristics. Thus the intuitive invention of animals differs radically from their purely instinctive reactions, and the intuitive physics of children and primitive men is a far cry from the intuitive understanding of chimpanzees which are merely aware of perceptual relations between the objects they handle. Similarly, man's tools, because of the way in which they are fashioned and also because of their multifarious purposes, are barely comparable with the ape's implements, which can hardly be said to be 'fashioned' at all, and which serve for only an immediate purpose. This discontinuity between the specific stages in the evolution of intelligence is due to the fact that each stage corresponds to a different level of mental development, each drawing on different types of knowledge. The continuity derived from activity is opposed by the discontinuity due to mental factors. The milestones in the evolution of intelligence are the emergence from instinctive reactions, and the appearance of conceptual thought. Both are roughly of equal importance: intelligence itself appearing in the first instance,

CONCLUSION

and the higher forms of thought in the second. If we really wish to put our finger on the dividing line between animals and men, we are most likely to discover it in the appearance of conceptual thought and speech.

This does not contradict Bergson's idea that man is characteristically a tool-maker. As we have pointed out, abstract thought plays a considerable part in human creativity, and everything goes to show that one of the distinctive characteristics of the tool (its universality) is due to the fact that it is constructed by a being capable of thinking in organised concepts. Conversely we have seen that practical intelligence is at the root of all rational discoveries. Thus the logical and the practical forms of man's intelligence complement each other, and this is the basis of all human progress.

It is a fact, however, that all men are not equally capable of developing these two forms of intelligence.

Quite possibly there are, or have been, races, epochs or even civilizations of a purely craftsman type and others of a purely intellectual type. Louis Weber, from whose interesting *Le Rhythme du Progrès* we have already quoted, holds that two predominant tendencies alternate cyclically in the history of human thought: the speculative and the technical. The first is marked by the influence of society, of language and of symbolic thought, the second by individual practical initiative. The exact phases of this periodic phenomenon would no doubt be difficult to determine. Technical intelligence would seem to have predominated in the Palaeolithic Age (flaked stone tools); the symbolic and speculative intelligence making its appearance with the mesolithic age (polished stone tools). Then, in the civilisations of ancient Egypt, and elsewhere in the East, there arose a new period of technical inventions, followed by a magnificent flowering of speculative intelligence in Greece. Later still, after the Middle Ages which brought a rebirth of practical intelligence, the Greek heritage was continued by the Renaissance. Today the speculative period of Western civilization would appear to be reaching its end, and to be giving way to that technical and highly scientific civilisation which is springing up before our very eyes.

Weber's theory is very tempting, and is certainly true in essence, if not in detail. Even if the changes are not as regular as the swing of the pendulum, it is a fact that the two tendencies exist, and that they can be observed in the differences between the everyday outlook and behaviour of the practical man and the theoretician. *Homo faber* survives within *Homo sapiens*, and his characteristic attributes are clearly demonstrated by those of us who combine both skill and mental ingenuity.

APPENDIX

For those who have neither the leisure nor the patience to solve the billiards problem (p. 110), I give the solution here in brief:

1. Consider first the case of *two balls and one cushion:* Draw the mirror image of the red ball *behind* the cushion and send the white ball towards it. It will be reflected so that it hits the red ball (a simple diagram will make this quite clear).

2. The case of *two balls and two cushions* (at right angles to each other): to determine the path of the white ball geometrically you must (a) find the mirror image of the red ball (first point) behind the second cushion, (b) find the mirror image of that point behind the first cushion, (c) direct the white ball towards that point. It will rebound to the first point and thence to the red ball.

3. The case of *two balls and three contiguous cushions:* Take the mirror image of the red ball behind the third cushion, then the mirror image of that point behind the second cushion, etc.

4. The case of *two balls and four cushions:* take the mirror image of the red ball in the third cushion, etc.

Clearly the final problem (cannon off all four cushions) cannot be solved directly, since it involves the simultaneous determination of the position of the vertices, and of the magnitude, of four angles which depend on one another. But the problem becomes a very simple matter when we apply the second and third Cartesian rules (the rules of *analysis* and *synthesis*), and when we assume that the solution of problem 1 (one cushion) will lead to the solution of problems 2, 3, and 4.

SELECT BIBLIOGRAPHY

ABERCROMBIE M. L. J.: *The Anatomy of Judgment* (1960).
BERGSON H.: *L'Evolution créatrice* (1902). *L' Effort intellectuel; L'Energie spirituelle* (1919).
BERNARD CL.: *Introduction to Experimental Medicine* (1927).
BINET A.: *L'Etude expérimentale de l'intelligence* (1903).
BOURDON B.: *L'Intelligence* (1926).
BOUTAN: *Les Deux méthodes de l'enfant* (Actes de la Societé Linnéenne de Bordeaux, vol. 68, 1914).
BOYCOTT B. B. and YOUNG J. Z.: *The Comparative Study of Learning* (Symp. Soc. Exp. Biol, 4, 1950).
BUYTENDIJK F. J.: *The Mind of the Dog* (1936).
DESCARTES R.: *Discours de la Méthode*.
DURKHEIM E.: *Formes élementaires de la vie religieuse* (1912).
ESPINAS A.: *Les Origines de la technologie* (1884).
FOX H. M.: *The Personality of Animals* (1940).
FRANCON J.: *The Mind of Bees* (1939).
GUILLAUME P.: *Psychologie des Singes* (Nouveau Traité de Psych. de G. DUMAS, vol. 8, 2). *La Psychologie animale* (1940). *Introduction à la Psychologie* (1942).
HALBWACHS M.: *Les Cadres sociaux de la memoire* (1925).
HARLOW H. and BROMER J.: *Comparative Behaviour of Primates* (Journ of Comp. Psych., Oct. 1939).
JAMES W.: *Principles of Psychology* (1890).
JANET (Dr. P.): *Les Débuts de l'intelligence* (1935). *L'Intelligence avant le langage* (1936).

KELLOG: *The Ape and the Child* (1933).
KOHLER W.: *The Mentality of Apes* (1925).
LANE F. W.: *Kingdom of the Octopus* (1957).
LEROI-GOURHAN A.: *L'Homme et la Nature* (Encyclopédie française, vol. 8). *L'Homme et la Matière* (1943). *Milieu et techniques* (1945).
LE ROY (Ed.): *Les Origines humaines et l'évolution de l'intelligence* 9L931).
LEVY-BRUHL: *La Mentalité primitive* (1922).
LUBBOCK, Sir J.: *Prehistoric Man* (1875). *On the Senses, Instincts and Intelligence of Animals* (1888).
MAIER N. R. F. and SCHNEIRLA T. C.: *Principles of Animal Psychology* (1935).
MORGAN J. DE: *L'Humanité prehistorique* (1937).
PIAGET J.: *La Representation du monde chez l'enfant* (1926). *La Psychologie de l'intelligence* (1947).
RENSCH B.: *Increase of Learning Capability with Increase of Brain-size* (The American Naturalist, Mar.-Apr. 1956). *The Intelligence of Elephants* (Scientific American, Feb. 1957).
REY A.: *L'intelligence pratique chez l'enfant* (1935).
SCHNEIRLA T. C.: *The Nature of Ant Learning* (Journ. of Comp. Psych., Apr. 1943).
TAINE: *L'Intelligence* (1870).
URABIN A.: *Psychologie des animaux sauvages* (1940).
WASHBURN M. F.: *The Animal Mind* (1936).
WEBER L.: *Le Rythme du Progrès* (1914).
WELLS H. G., HUXLEY J. and WELLS G. P.: *The Science of Life* (1930).
WOODWORTH R. S.: *Experimental Psychology* (1938).

INDEX

INDEX

Aborigines, 59, 89f
Actogram, 51f
Altamera caves, 93
Animal Intelligence, 25ff
Approach Impulse, 12
Archimedes, 59
Avoidance, 12

Bernard, Claude, 94
Bergson, H., 10, 21, 55, 82f, 86f, 100, 102, 117
Billiard problem, 110f
Binet, A., 72
Blondel, C., 20
Boomerang, 59
Bourdon, 72
Boutan, 22, 41, 43f, 80
Byzantine civilisation, 94

Canguilhem, G., 58
Causality, 99f
Chellean culture, 62
Chinese civilization, 94
Claparède, E., 18, 93, 111
Codrington, C., 90
Comte, A., 81, 86
Conceptual Thought, 19f, 53, 71ff

Descartes, 12, 19, 109ff
Detour problems, 27
Drescher, 30
Durkheim, E., 89f
Dynamic Scheme, 83

Egocentric mentality, 90f
Empiricism, 101f
Eskimos, 59, 65, 68
Espinas, A., 57f
Experimental psychology, 26

Fabre, J., 13f

General Tendency, 66f
Gestalt psychology, 74
Gottschaldt, 22, 42, 44
Guillaume, P., 22, 31, 36, 45, 53, 64, 89

Hadamard, J., 111
Halbwachs, M., 83f
Harlow, 29
Head, 85
Hoe experiment, 45f
Hume, D., 89

Imagination, 81ff
Infantile mentality, 96f

Instinct, 11, 13f, 35
Invention, 26f, 57f
Iroquois, 90

James, W., 13
Janet, P., 10
Johnson, 72

Kanakas, 61, 68
Kant, 95
Kapp, E., 58
Kellog, 41
Kipling, 56
Köhler, W., 16f, 22, 27f, 31f, 38f, 41, 44, 47, 55f, 57, 84f

Language, 19f, 22, 53, 74ff
Lapps, 65, 68
Lecène, P., 94
Leenhard, 62, 68
Lefebvre-Desnonelles, 59f, 62, 63
Leroi-Gourhan, A., 57, 59, 65, 66f
Le Roy, E., 21
Lévy-Bruhl, L., 21, 89, 90, 94
Locke, J., 89
Locomotion Problems, 28f
Loeb, 11
Logical Intelligence, 28f, 71ff

Meillet, A., 88f
Melanesians, 90
Memory, 81ff
Meyersohn, 22, 31, 45

Mill, J. S., 89
Morgan, J. de, 59, 61f
Mystical Causality, 96f

Objectivity, 99f

Pacific Tribes, 104
Palaeolithic age, 118
Pappus of Alexandria, 59, 109
Paramecium, 15
Pascal, 19
Participation, 96f
Percussion, 62f, 67f
Piaget, J., 72, 89, 90ff, 97
Plato, 109
Poincaré, H., 82
Practical Intelligence, 20, 41ff, 55ff, 85
Prehension, 29
Primitive mentality, 96f
Psychology of Tool-making, 58

Rabaud, 17
Rational Intelligence, 88ff, 95ff
Reflexes, 11
Reindeer Age, 59
Rey, A., 22, 47ff, 57
Rudder, 60

Settlage, 29
Stern, 91, 93
Solring Problems, 106f

Taine, 72, 89
Taton, R., 111
Tools, 55ff, 58, 101f
Trendelenburg, 30
Tropisms, 11f

Urbain, M., 37

Vinacke, 72
Voltaire, 20

Weber, L., 21, 117f
Wommera, 58f
Woodworth, R. S., 72

Yerkes, 22, 42

BF
431
.V513
1973

CANISIUS COLLEGE LIBRARY
BUFFALO, N. Y.